The Complete
Male Handbook

for

Sex, Dating, and Other Trivial Stuff

The Complete
Male Handbook

for

Sex, Dating, and Other Trivial Stuff

By

Peter Bartula

toExcel

San Jose New York Lincoln Shanghai

The Complete Male Handbook
for
Sex, Dating, and Other Trivial Stuff

Published by toExcel, an imprint of iUniverse.com, Inc.

For information address:
iUniverse.com, Inc.
620 North 48th Street, Suite 201
Lincoln, NE 68504
www.iuniverse.com

ISBN: 1-58348-295-4

LCCN: 99-63460

Printed in the United States of America

To Kelly—My Wife, My Muse, and a Major Part of My Life

Foreword

I would imagine that the average reader will scan this page for a list of the qualifications that enabled me to write a book about the complex topics of sex and dating. Have I done an exhaustive survey of the American population analyzing contemporary dating habits with a margin of error of plus or minus 2 percent? Do I have a Ph.D. in sociology, human sexuality, or even psychology (actually I slept more during my token sociology and psychology courses in college than I did in bed, but then again didn't everybody?) Do I at least have a sexual history that would make Wilt Chamberlain's claim of 10,000+ sexual encounters pale in comparison? Well, to be honest, the answer to all of those questions is, well, um, uh, no.

But don't chuck this book in the recycling bin with last week's sports section just yet. The next 150 pages will provide you with a veritable plethora of tips on dating, love, and the pursuit of the ideal woman from a guy who has been in the "game" more years than Nolan Ryan. If you are currently single (hence the reason that you have enough idle time on your hands to be reading this book), you will probably pick up some ideas and insights that will help you on your quest to find Ms. Perfect. Even if you don't, you'll take pride in knowing that you are not the only one who hasn't mastered the art of molding the perfect woman, and you'll be able to empathize with some of my faceplants and temporary successes in the dating world. You'll probably even come away with a few laughs and one-liners as you journey through the following chapters. However, if you find this book so enlightening that you use it as your personal dating textbook, I, the publisher, and your local bookstore take no responsibility for any physical, emotional, or genital damages that you may incur by following the suggestions contained within this book.

At any rate, just remember that the right woman could be a beer away next Friday night, so take a tip from someone who's been there and keep on plugging away.

Contents

A Slice of the Life

An Inside Look at a Typical Weekend

What does "an average guy's" guide to sex and dating mean? How do I define myself as being an average guy? To help shed some light on what makes me Mr. Middle-of-the-Road, I'll detail one of my typical weekends to help you gain perspective on my attitudes and how I view the topics of dating and sex. Just for the record, currently I'm not seeing anyone on a regular basis. ("regular basis" is defined as longer than the duration of the average hangover.) Don't get me wrong; I am looking to find something more long-term. But until someone comes along who meets my dating standards, I'm hard at work in the dog-eat-dog world that is the singles scene. It has been about eight months since my last girlfriend. While I haven't gotten to the "I'll take anyone that eats, breathes, and doesn't wet the bed" stage yet, I am intensifying my search to find someone with whom I could spend more than 12 hours. But I'm starting to get ahead of myself. Without further ado, let the fun begin.

Ahhh, the weekend. Time for two straight days of fun, irresponsibility, and uninhibited frolic. Not much that is worthy of the excitement files occurs during the typical work week, so on my two day reprieve from "9 to 5" I strive to make up for the five days of semi-blasé. At a bare minimum, it's almost always a pile of fun. Tonight's agenda will take us to our most recent bar du' jour, a place called *Big Boppers*. It's not a place to meet the woman of your dreams, but tonight I don't want dreams. I want to hang-out with some friends, tip a few back, bark like a dog, and see if I can meet someone—who I'd still be happy with in the morning. That doesn't seem to be too much to ask for on a Friday night, does it?

The bar's crowd varies considerably in the age categor, from women who were already old when the Big Bopper was popular, to those who weren't even born then. Given my current state of mind, I'd be willing to venture forth on an evening's journey with a woman in either category. That's not to suggest that my life is *totally* dictated by my testosterone level. But, until I find the woman that sweeps me off my feet, I'm keeping my options open. This open attitude allows me to meet a lot of women, and also has given me a few stories that would make Hugh Hefner blush. Most of my friends have the same attitudes and virtues (or lack thereof), so it's not difficult to manage a good time. If nothing else, the bar life usually makes for some humorous hangover stories over a Saturday morning bowl of Captain Crunch. However, I'm finding that as we pass our mid twenties, the number of compatriots in this carefree category is quickly diminishing. Another one is taking the plunge into matrimony next month—another tux rental, another big party, another night of prospecting for a 12-hour-hook-up, all the while secretly wanting to be the one taking the leap for a lifetime.

I guess marriage is the phase of human evolution beyond my current lifestyle. You can only spend so many years partying, having one night sex sessions, and waking up under the neighbor's tree with a skull-crushing headache before you start to wonder if there isn't something more to life. That's when people say "What the hell, marriage is something different, why not try it?" It will happen to me too, someday. (Not tonight, mind you, but someday.) I wouldn't mind marriage, though. I have my lonely nights and times that I miss not having a steady relationship. I'm sure that there is a woman out there who will make my heart go pitter-patter. As of now she has yet to appear, so I'll keep pushing on through the endless acres of weeds looking for a flower among them. If I don't find her, at least I'll enjoy myself right here and now—strolling through my field of dreams. Maybe I'll even wake up under a tree again.

Upon arriving at Boppers, I am quickly greeted by a 42-year-old woman who my friends affectionately call "Grandma." I met her a couple of weeks back when a friend's drunken dare caused me to ask "Ms. Middle-Aged" to dance. She's not Jane Fonda, but her parts still look toned and shapely. Her only sign of advanced years are a couple of crow's feet that line her eyes, but I'm not looking to put a ring on her finger…besides, you don't see crows feet in the dark.

On the night we met, she told me that I moved better than anyone she ever danced with. That was enough of an ego stroke for me to buy her a drink and spend some time talking with her after we'd finished dancing. During the ensuing conversation I discovered that she had a laid-back-yet-pleasing personality. She was recently divorced, and it was obvious that she was looking to latch onto a new companion before the dust settled on the other side of her bed. Given her attitudes on life and her ongoing partner search, it seemed she was riding on the same social boat as I was, but with a 20-year headstart.

Our conversation went smoothly until we hit a brick wall while discussing our goals for the evening. She made the mistake of asking me about my interests. Being the suave, and never-subtle person that I am, "I'm interested in sex," seemed to be the appropriate response.

She said she was into "commitment." To which I replied "I'm committed to sex."

She was not overly impressed, but she laughed politely. I guess my honesty and forwardness took her off guard. Unfortunately, it didn't get me anywhere that night. On to the next woman.

I enjoy talking with older women. They usually have more personality than their less aged counterparts and the fact that they don't use the word "like" as punctuation in a normal conversation is a refreshing change from most bar conversations. There are only so many times that you can handle hearing about what's on sale in the "Women's Wear Section" at the local mall's department stores. Some evening-long late-night chats with older women have taught me things about myself or provided me with some insightful observations about life, an unexpected "Bonus Prize" from my average Friday night game show.

That night was the fourth time that I'd seen "Grandma." I'd always managed some creative quips to keep her curiosity piqued, and it seemed that she enjoyed the attention of a younger guy. After greeting me with a big hug, she introduced me to her friend saying that "This is the guy that I told you about." Then "Ms. 42-and-shapely" proceeded to ask me "What am I going to do with you?"

"I can think of a few things," I replied in my usual character.

"I think I might take you up on your offer."

This wasn't the same "commitment" woman that I met a month ago, was it? What caused this 180 degree turn around? Maybe she was getting lonely, or maybe she was getting soured on her search for Mr. Right, who knows. It was good to know that if all else failed, there was still a potential partner for the evening on the horizon.

My friends appeared to need a pep talk, so it was time for some social drinking and a bit of conversation with the team. That night my beverage of choice was rum and orange juice. It gets the job done quicker than beer and gets me that recommended daily allowance of Vitamin C that the '90s nutrition gurus preach so strongly about. (Also I knew the barmaid, so I got the drinks served to me at industrial strength.) This is usually an advantage, but that particular drink tasted more like hi-grade motor oil than something you'd purposely ingest. I put up with it, a little extra liquid-courage never hurt anybody. Through my years of experience with the bar scene, I've found that self-confidence is raised and pickiness is lowered exponentially with every drink above and beyond the fourth. This is a big plus when scouring for women along with 50 other confident young guys who all share a common goal for the evening.

The conversation with the guys followed a fairly standard list of topics. Girls. The baseball game on TV, girls, what things we wanted to do with the beautiful girl in the corner wearing the orange dress, then more talk about girls. At least we were focused.

After the usual quota of conversation time, we decided to make the inevitable "lap around the bar." An attractive girl in a floral dress was the best prospect on lap #1, but a smile and a quick "hi" were the extent of my efforts up to that point. The lap conveniently finished at a location in the bar which allowed me to stare at the floral woman with an unobstructed view. Back to talking with the guys, until the opportunity presented itself.

The DJ's next music selection was a slow song, and the motor-oil drink had done its job. That combination was enough to put me in a state of readiness for the challenge of finding a woman to get acquainted with. Some guy who looked more like one of the floral woman's past elementary school teachers than a potential date asked her to dance, but she politely declined. Time for the guy wearing my shoes to make his move. I started slow—a blatant stare, cocked head, and a confident smile. As luck would have it, she noticed these "not-so coy" signals and motioned for me to meet her on the dance floor.

Now this was not a regular occurrence for me. I never complain when good looking women ask me to dance, but it doesn't happen every day. My looks don't get me on any magazine covers nor do they give 18 year-olds a mad case of the raging thigh sweats, though I would say that I'm on the better side of average-looking. I try to supplement that with a sense of humor and self-confidence. Whatever it was, the floral woman seemed interested.

After enduring three elbows in the face, four "excuse me's" and one near fatal Budweiser bath while plowing through the crowd, I finally made it to her. After the normal introductions, we ventured out onto the dance floor—the social proving ground of the adult world. A slow dance can make or break the bar-frequenting male. Extra care in what to say and do here are of the utmost importance. Fortunately, it took only a few seconds before she had me locked in a tight embrace. That gave my roving hands the opportunity to get an initial reading on the Cellulite-o-meter. My first "trip" down her back felt softer than both a baby's butt and expensive toilet paper combined. From this I determined that body-wise, she was more than dateable. I also got a pretty good approximation of her body measurements (give or take an inch) should it ever come up in casual discussion. Following my exploration she showed her interest by pressing close enough to me to remove even the most stubborn wrinkles from my shirt. We spiced up our adult merry-go-round ride by adding some conversation to begin the process of getting to know each other. After our eighth circle, I had a rough assessment of her personality. She was about a 6 on a 1-to-10 scale. She seemed more nice than fun, and (if you haven't guessed by now) I am just the opposite. She also had a very unusual dichotomy in her life. She was an accountant, but she lived on a farm 25 miles out of town, keeping a farmer's hours and hobbies. What a picture—milk old Bessie, fetch some eggs, then off to work for some income statements and balance sheets with a couple of corporate stuffed shirts. Different, but who was I to question. She also had me by three candles on life's birthday cake. I didn't have a problem with that, but the two kids that were the pride and joy of her life did move her a bit lower on my list.

Instead of my usual next moves of buying her a drink and continuing our conversation, I put her in the hopper for later. She'd probably have to go home and take over for the 16-year-old baby-sitter at midnight anyway. The distance, the kids, and the lack of exceptional personality kept her out of the relationship category, but just in case no one better came along, I left her in the bedtime ball game. Maybe I'd give her another at bat later. At any rate, I'd been at the bar for 20 minutes, and I had two potential contestants for the "Take-Me-Home-and-Undress-Me" contest.

My friends weren't having as much success. No dancing, not even a casual conversation yet. But, I usually need the least time and buzz to get flowing. Time to go back to the safety net of the guy circle and rally the troops. Also, another glass of motor oil wouldn't hurt.

As I stood there and looked at the people around me, I realized one thing that has always struck me as funny about bars. People put on their best clothes, psyche themselves into their best mood of the week, and spend a large portion of their free evenings at a strange place to stand around drinking, talking, and staring at people. All for the hope of meeting the one person that will change his/her life, and delve them into a world of love and romance. Of the eight years and 500 or so trips to bars that I have made, this has yet to happen for me. Granted, I've had some great sexual experiences, a lot of fond memories, and immeasurable quantities of laughter and friendships out of it. But I have yet to come even close to accomplishing my major objective.

So is this path that I run down most every weekend the right one? Or, is it just leading me further away from the pot of gold that I'm after? It seems to be a lot like playing the lottery. Your chances of winning are about a gazillion to one, but you keep playing every week because there's "always that chance" that next time you'll win. The odds are low, but the reward is a lot higher than the investment. All you need is a dollar and a dream.

Are we all just trying too hard to hit the romance jackpot? I've found in my end-less travels that when you're searching too desperately for something, you will never find it. It's an attitude thing. Women have a sixth sense about guys, sort of like how a Doberman senses your fear that he will soon gnaw off one of your vital limbs. If you have a look of desperation, you'll crash and burn every time. Maybe that's part of the reason that I tell myself that I'm just looking to have a good time when I go out. Chances are that I'd be 0 for 501 in my bar room quest to meet the woman of my dreams after another Friday night.

Maybe there's something that I'm missing here? But how do you know what is the correct way to meet the right woman? No one I've ever met had the perfect recipe for falling in love. Even people that have succeeded in finding the person who is "the one" for them will tell you they don't know how it happened. They are, however, always more than happy to give you that trite token piece of advice—"just be your-self and it will happen." I think that there's a law on the books somewhere that when you fall in love you have to spout that ridiculous line to all of your single friends each time you see them. It's supposed to comfort us in the fact that there is supposedly someone out there above the personal attractiveness of a barn-yard animal who might actually have some interest in you. In actuality it causes you to slide closer to depres-sion knowing that someone who used to carouse for women with you, now has found someone nice enough to turn Jack the Ripper into a Ginsu Chef, while your only suc-cesses are in meeting toothless women with IQ's hovering painfully close to their age.

A few minutes further into my festive Friday, woman number three entered the picture. She was a 30-something year-old that I met at Boppers a couple of weeks back. She was a fairly attractive blonde divorcee who easily passed the looks test with my friends. This is a simple test consisting of a simultaneous utterance of the phrase "I'd do her" when she turned her back to them. Her personality works and she doesn't have any major flaws. The age thing is a slight drawback but what the heck, "I'd do her."

I was supposed to take her wine-tasting a few weeks back, but we didn't go. She didn't impress me an incredible amount, and there was a great football game on the tube that day. So I weighed my alternatives and blew her off. It would have been over right then, but I got horny a week later and called her back. I blew her off again later that week, but I straightened both situations out with a couple of well-placed creative explanations.

Now for the usual routine: a couple of dances, a few drinks, and a few laughs. Then comes the more difficult part of trying to get out of the bar for some extra-curricular activities. Amazingly enough she was still interested in me, and everything proceeded according to the Friday night game plan. Her body language told me that taking her home was in the cards. Conversation revealed that she was divorced from a dominant husband who abused her. The emotion in her voice showed me that she still wore the scars of that situation, but her interest in me showed that she was ready to move on. Throughout the conversation I made sure to show that I was sympathetic to her problem while simultaneously promoting my cause. This was essential if I was going to have a chance to make my play with her. I balanced her needs with mine very well. Now came crunch time.

I asked her if she wanted to leave. She replied in the affirmative, so I readied myself to meet and exceed my goals for the evening. There was still another hour of bar time, but I was quickly running out of things to keep our conversation rolling. I told the friends that I was heading out and gave them a smile that boasted, "I've found someone to take home tonight and you haven't."

When I walked her to her car and informed her that I didn't drive, the body language and signals did a complete reversal. All of a sudden she turned into Sybil, Rambo, and Satan all rolled into one. Realizing that I was expecting her to drive me back to my place for some physical endeavors, she backed off and gave me the "I don't do that with people I don't know" routine. A bunch of smoothing over, a long kiss good-bye, and a date for later in the week was the best that I could do. Even my best five minute selling job to get her to change her mind didn't work. I pulled a couple of "but I really like you" and "nothing will happen, I just want to get to know you better" lines, but neither helped me make the sale. A lost cause, I went back to the bar to find the other two women.

Upon returning to the bar and finding my friends, they gave me the necessary quota of abuse and ridicule about striking out with her. This is an important part of the male bonding process that occurs whenever a friend falls short of his objectives for the evening. When there's an opening to get a shot in at someone you have to hit him with it. In this group, when a man's down, you always make sure to kick him.

They also informed me that both "Grandma" and Ms. Floral left after giving me the evil eye for talking to the psycho-kiss-and-a-date woman. My choice of women for the evening was about as successful as the nautical career of the captain of the Titanic, but "C'est la vie." The only saving grace was that there was still another twenty minutes of bar time left.

Unfortunately, a quick perusal of the available women, coupled with a high level of standards from my waning buzz, put a nix on the possibility of finding someone else. Time to pack it up for the night, go get some food at a sleazy local diner, and rehash the night's details like fishing stories about the one that got away.

After the Friday night washout let's move the calendar ahead a day. Saturday. Time for round two of the weekend festivities. Just for a change of pace we decided to throw a party at the homestead. Parties are good. It's easier to hook-up with someone at a party than in a bar because being at someone's home lowers everyone's level of apprehension about meeting people. You might go to a bar with a group of guys and see a pack of girls who promptly tell you that you are about as attractive as a three-foot chancre sore, but given the same group of people at a party, you would hook-up. At a party there's an atmosphere that you're a friend versus being just another sleazeball at a bar trying to get laid. In about the same number of outings at each, my success rate is double at parties versus bars. I was hopeful that this party wouldn't be an exception.

To give you some background on my living arrangements, our house is like the movie "Three Men and a Baby" except we don't have a kid. We're three financially secure bachelors under one roof with women coming in and out the doors with a level of regularity that would put Metamucil to shame. Hence the nickname "Sin Central," has graced our house. Usually our parties don't come equipped with enough women to find a perfect female, but there are certainly enough to make it worthwhile. The crop of women at this gathering was much the same. As an ace-in-the-hole, I invited one that I had a sexual past with. I was certainly prepared. My childhood boy-scout training actually did me some good after all.

Beer, guys, girls, drinking games, sex. That's a party in its lowest common denominator. Maybe more sophisticated types may have wine, cheese and conversations that could change the world as we know it, but I've gone both routes and I think that sticking to the basics wins out. It may seem more like a college fraternity party than a party of people in their mid-twenties with respectable jobs, but I've always hung around with a group that worries more about having fun than trying to impress people. We like it that way, and the girls here don't complain.

The time-frame of these gatherings is fairly standardized: an hour of people arriving and entering into mild socializing, two or three hours of a more hard-core brand of party, followed by an hour of people discretely disappearing two by two into various dark corners of the house, never to be heard from for the remainder of the evening. The pre-existing couples and married people file out during this period, and the guys that didn't couple up eventually drink themselves into oblivion on the nearest piece of furniture. Before passing out, however, they achieve a great phenomenon in the universe known as the "drunken derelict dialogue." These incoherent conversations that occur between the people of the big buzz are barely remembered in the morning. They never cover anything above 4th-grade level but serve an important function by allowing their participants to feel that they are not as useless as breasts on a bowling ball, despite the fact that none of the girls at the party would have anything to do with them. Having been an occasional participant in said conversations, I have had good insight into their subject matter.

Now for the dynamics of a party pick-up. During phase one of the party, you have to make yourself noticed. When you do this, you have to be careful not to be too aggressive or obnoxious. This is tough for me because I usually like to be the focus of attention. I purposely hold back, go for some safe jokes, and say a few lines where appropriate.

As the social drinking process gets rolling, it is time to step things up a bit. You start to notice that the females are getting much more attention in the conversation at this point and this is when I choose to make a few sexually risqué comments. Right from the beginning of this stage you can catch the little signals of who is interested in whom, and where to direct your attention. The touch signal is usually a good indicator. Unless a girl is really a touchy-feely type, a touch of a hand on a shoulder or a slap on a shoulder for a crude remark usually guarantees a hook-up if you play your cards right. I like drinking games at parties because they give you a good idea of who a girl is interested in by noticing who she doles out her drinking "penalties" to.

Being a bit hornier and lazier that night, I took the ace-in-the-hole right from the start. I was careful to leave the option for future sex with her open the last time I saw her for just that reason. We don't call each other, we don't date, but we both have a great time together. Whenever we're at a party together, we always end up in the bedroom.

In the party's drinking phase I proceeded to get a bit beyond the normal level of intoxication. Being the center of attention causes you to get more inebriated than the average person, but that's fine because my lock on my prospect for the evening was as strong as the aroma of stale beer would be in the living room the next morning.

As the time neared where buzz and hormones were to collide, a moment of tension occurred. Asking a girl to leave her friends (and look a bit cheap in the process) to go into a bedroom and have sex can be a bit touchy. I have no set technique or line that I use at this moment, but the simple "I wanna make love to you!" worked this time. That statement in itself is a facade since there isn't a shred of love involved in what we were about to do, but girls prefer that terminology because it makes the act sound less degrading. Whatever it took, I was there.

Now came the part I'd waited for. It had been about a month since my last encounter, so I was especially happy about what I was about to indulge in. The first place that I took her to was my bedroom, but unfortunately an opportunistic pair of partygoers eliminated that option. The fact that two people were having sex in my bed would have normally pissed me off, but with impending sex on my mind I dismissed my anger and remained focused on the matter at hand.

We wound up in a sleeping bag on the floor of the laundry room. Not my preferred location for casual sex, but it would have to do. Being a guy (even worse, a horny-drunk guy), my natural instinct was to cut through the red tape and get right to the act itself. Foreplay of "are your clothes off, yet?" might have occurred on a drunken one night stand, but this situation was a bit different. Having some respect and a genuine compassion for the person that I was about to be with, made me feel as though I owed it to her to spend some time easing into the act.

I took some time going through the various sex stages and gave each body part the proper time to ready itself for the big event. It's comparable to getting the proper daily intake of the four food groups—minimum quantities of time are important for what I call the four sex areas: 1) above the shoulders, 2) shoulders to waist, 3) the area right next door, 4) nirvana. The fourth area produces the most intense physical pleasure, but given the normal course of sexual activity, the time spent here is usually the shortest. Given the amount of alcohol I took in that night the time that we experienced nirvana was a bit longer. In case you're having trouble figuring this one out, consult with a physician or with any male that has attempted sex while drunk. They'll clue you in.

The foreplay and the sex itself where both good. Siskel and Ebert would have definitely given her two thumbs-up. But then again if you've ever looked at Siskel and Ebert, they would probably give just about anyone that would sleep with them that sign of praise. This girl was a moaner—something all guys love. The boost to the ego and the feeling that you are bringing such intense pleasure to a woman to make her produce those sounds are big pluses in a sex experience.

This girl was different from most. In almost all non-love sex encounters, the girl is pretty tame. Not saying that guys are sexual dynamos, but girls are generally not that active during casual sex. Maybe they just save the good stuff for serious relationships. It's an unspoken female law that they must hold back on the primo sex until their hooks are firmly entrenched in the man. That will help to suck us men into love, so that we can get the "rip-my-clothes-off-and-make-me-see-God" sex. But whatever the case, this girl definitely violated the female code, because she was like a 15-year pro-football veteran—she gave 110% every time and played only for the love of the game.

You're probably wondering why I don't go out with her on a permanent basis. We do have a good time together and the sex is definitely great. I just don't feel the special spark with her that separates someone that I enjoy being with from a woman that I can fall in love with. I can't put my finger on what it is about her that doesn't cut it, but I do know that it's not there with her, nor would it ever be.

It's too bad because she really deserved to have someone that she could have fallen in love with. She should have someone who would take her to the nice restaurants and fritter away whole paychecks on a single date. I know our relationship kept her from having that to some extent. Maybe she was like me, looking for the right one and enjoying some casual sex until she found the right person. At any rate, she moaned, I breathed heavy, and there were no strings attached. It was a good thing.

After a single prolonged sex session, she had to depart. That was also a good thing. As a drunk male, the millisecond after the sex act culminated, going to sleep was all that I thought about. I think someone should do some research and study ejaculation as a cure for male insomnia. It is guaranteed to induce extreme drowsiness every time. After dressing, walking her to her car, and a customary kiss goodbye, I was destined only to crawl into bed and not awaken until sometime Sunday afternoon.

But alas, one thing stood between me and that pillow. The four drunk guys who didn't hook-up had gathered in the living room. Combined, they were the equivalent to the Fearsome Foursome of the LA Rams football fame. I, being a lowly running back, had no chance of getting to the bed zone without a few beers and some useless conversation.

Rather than fight an endless verbal barrage in an attempt to make it through their defense, I relented, grabbed a beer and began telling them the only thing they cared about—details! Frustrated from being passed by in the sex game, they found solace and peace of mind in hearing about someone else's sexcapades. Again, being a man of the people who wants everyone to be happy, and also being someone who doesn't mind giving himself an occasional pat on the back, I gave in to their wishes.

After I filled my conversation and beer requirement, I was then able to pass through them like Jim Brown. But with some beer back in my system, and the adrenaline of 20 minutes of juicy story telling behind me, the thought of the cold pillow greeting my face didn't seem as appealing. It was time to move on to a higher drunken pursuit.

Yes, it was time to make sure Ma Bell's quarterly profits remained high enough to protect my grandfather's only stock investment. It was time to reach out and touch someone. Because I have good friends in many different places throughout the country, my checkbook isn't too fond of this ritual. At 3 a.m. on Sunday morning, waking them up to inform them that I'm drunk is a better option than getting those necessary eight hours sleep. I once considered putting a breathalyzer on the phone after receiving a monthly long-distance bill for a $150. The device would be simple, if I blow above .08 BAC, I wouldn't be able to get a dial-tone. This feature would save me about $50 a month, and would make the weekend early morning hours much more peaceful for my friends. But, it would certainly be less entertaining for everyone—most importantly me.

The night's lucky contestant in the "Awakened from a Deep Sleep by An Obnoxious Drunk" Game was my friend Julie in Boston. She's been one of my close friends for a couple of years, and we have a great relationship. I can tell her about my weekend endeavors without needing to take a gallon of whitewash to them as I would with most females, and in the course of our conversations, she told me about what was happening in her life as well.

I met Julie in my first year of grad school. My initial thoughts were that I immediately wanted the wedding, the 2.5 kids, and the dog named Spot in the backyard—the whole nine yards. She has all of the take home-to-mom qualities. The looks, the brains, the sense of humor, and the personality all got straight A's in my book. My plans got screwed up when she got involved in a pseudo relationship with my best friend. After that I realized that my chances with her were "a snowball's in hell," but I liked talking and spending time with her so much that we developed a platonic relationship. For me a friendship with a girl without ever entertaining thoughts of sex is like passing through allergy season without a single sneeze. A synapse must have misfired somewhere, and now there we were.

The strange thing about our relationship is how two very different types of people associate with each other as close friends. She is shy, quiet, and goes out of her way to please people, and I'm outgoing, wild, and please people when it fits my cause. Since I've known her I've noticed that she reeks of upper-class values and attitudes, but she's never snotty and she never puts herself above anyone else. She's more cosmopolitan and artsy than I am, but we're both open-minded and willing to learn from each other. Surprisingly, her "do the right thing" attitude actually attracted me to her and has served as a stabilizing force in my life whenever I venture too far into the deep end. Throughout our friendship, she's been my barometer of life's rights and wrongs, and most of the time I follow her advice.

Three years later and 300 miles apart, we still talk once every few weeks. Lately though, we've even added a new facet to our friendship. Whenever we talk it ends up being a tell-all of our recent exploits as single people in the modern world. Her methods for looking for the perfect mate are much different, more moral, and less exciting than mine, but she always was a bit more sedate. After I shared my stories of wine and women without sparing any details, she informed me that she lived life vicariously through me. She gets the lurid details and a taste of life on the other side without the risks to life, limb, property, and sanity.

That night's talk was no different. My weekend endeavors satisfied her appetite to see life on the wild side, and I (despite drunken state of mind) was, as always, interested in hearing her more tame, yet interesting, tidbits of life. Despite the differences, we always found some insights into our lives and to dating that seemed equally applicable to both of us. The conversation made me realize even more that despite the high fun quota that my lifestyle provided me, I was truly looking to find something more.

After I hung-up the phone with her I finally felt satisfied in my weekend pursuits—sex, fun, partying, and even a couple of personal revelations. Now I could hit the sheets with no weights on my shoulders and a grin on my face.

So do you think that I am a wretched, sexist, waste of human flesh after reading about my typical weekend endeavors? Most females and a few "holier than moi'" males are probably in the "yes" category. This is the life that I have chosen to lead at this point, and I'm pretty happy with it. I realize that it is not even close to being politically correct, but until I find a woman who can change this, it works for me. I know that entering a serious relationship with a woman would cure me of many of my immoral habits while adding stability to my life. That is why I am seeking this, despite my continuing pursuits that run on the contrary. So why haven't I found what I want? Maybe I'm looking in the wrong places. Maybe I don't know what I want in a woman. Who knows? I guess that before I can find the woman of my dreams, I should figure out what I'm looking for, and the best place to find such a person. This is as good a starting place as any on the road to a long-term relationship.

The Fantasy Mate

What To Look For In a Woman

Now you know the color of the sky in my world. It's usually a great time, but for the long haul I'm definitely looking for something different. I'd like to find a woman to sweep off her feet, to spend time with, and to do the many things in life that you can only do with a partner. More so, I'm searching for someone with whom I can share my life, grow old with, and live happily ever after.

So let's delve into dreamland and come up with someone who is Cindy Crawford, Mother Theresa, and my mom all rolled into one—now there's a woman! I will attempt this, knowing full well that the constraints placed upon me by my average physical appearance and ordinary personality would never allow me to actually find and do the nuptials thing with such a woman. At least you will get an idea of what I'm looking for.

My disclaimers to the things on this list are that I'm not omnipotent, my opinions are not impervious to change, and I'm not even in possession of a balanced moral structure. As you read this chapter, compare these attributes to what you feel is important and compile your own personal scorecard. You'll be surprised to find out what qualities are important to you, and it will help to give you some insight as to what you are looking for. These qualities vary substantially from man to man, but this is what works for me at this moment in time.

Here is my so called "top 10 list", weighted by order of importance. (A drum roll please!)

1. Physical appearance

I know, the female contingent is going to get all over my case for putting physical appearance above all else, but think about it for a minute. Appearance is the first thing that you notice about someone. The woman with the perfect personality will never even get to the plate if she has the body and face of Rin-Tin-Tin. Yes, call me superficial, but if I'm going to have a romantic attraction to someone, I will have it with the whole package. A big part of this package is the physical appearance of the person you'll be staring at when you're together. It's holding a hand that doesn't have cellulose engulfing yours. It's being able to kiss a face that doesn't have liquid oozing from every pore. I've heard the arguments and overused clichés that people use about appearance. Love is blind. Beauty is only skin deep. You can't judge a book by it's cover—take your pick. These things may be true, but when you first meet someone, your blindness hasn't set in yet, and if there is no physical attraction when you begin the relationship, you may never feel that initial infatuation that helps to set her apart from any other woman walking down the street.

I'm not saying that I'll only marry a Miss America contestant, but I think everyone has a minimum appearance standard that their mate must meet. Mine may be higher or lower than that of other people, but at least I acknowledge that it exists.

One of my older brothers once told me, that if people don't have enough respect for themselves to keep healthy, chances are that they have an inherent laziness or personal deficiency that could hinder the relationship in the long run. If a woman is going to kick the bucket 10 years before me and leave me alone to rot in an old folks home because she couldn't pry herself away from the bonbons, my life won't be as fulfilling as it could be. I don't want to spend the bulk of my gray days playing checkers with some burly guy named Max. That's not my idea of maximizing my enjoyment of life. Also, the many physical activities that we could do together would be limited if the old ball and chain can't participate due to physical constraints. If I can't ski, play tennis, or exercise with the company of the Mrs., that's a big X in the negative column for her.

Now here comes the cover-my-butt disclaimer. I know that physical appearance shouldn't play a major role in determining your mate. For me it is merely one part of the big picture, but it is nonetheless an important part. But, cut me some slack, I am fantasizing.

As long as I am, and since we are discussing physical appearance here, let me build you the fantasy woman. In the height category she should be between 5' and 5'5". I'd like a small women, and she must be shorter than I am so we don't look like Paul Simon and one of his dates when we're together at social gatherings. I also like a petite body with a flattering roundness in the upper and lower areas that males often get caught staring at. By preferring this body type, I differ from most of my male counterparts in that I'm not a fanatic about large breasts. If they happen to be planted on a petite frame, I'll take them. But I prefer breasts that fit into the medium-size category. The face for my dream woman would be an apple pie, no-make-up-necessary complexion—someone who doesn't need to do a Tammy Faye Baker make-up routine before I can look at her in the morning. Put that with any hair color, red being of last choice, and the personality qualities yet to be outlined, and you have my woman to grow old with.

2. Sense of humor

To me this is the most important personality trait. A girl could steal everything I own, sleep with everyone on my block, and commit gross bodily function faux pas in public on a regular basis, but if she can make me laugh non-stop, I'm hooked. Of course, she also has to tolerate and appreciate my "fine" (but certainly not refined) sense of humor, because I definitely get along better with people who can share my laughter.

One of the best feelings (not as good as sex or taking off your ski boots at the end of the day mind you, but still good) is laughing until you cry with someone. I had a dinner date as a first date with a great woman about a year back. Before the appetizer course was even on the table, we had four separate groups of fellow restaurant patrons giving us death stares because of our uncontrolled laughter. The waitress, who definitely picked the wrong table to have as her first ever, was terrified. To top it all off, during the salad course, a bacon bit flew out of my mouth when she caught me off guard with a punchline. Rather than turning a deeper shade of red than a horror movie victim, I looked at her and we stepped-up our laughter a couple of decibels. Talk about a great way to ease first-date tensions and warm up to a person in a hurry. I was so impressed with her that I ended up taking her to see the *Phantom of the Opera* that weekend. Unfortunately, soon after blowing vast amounts of money on her, her ex-boyfriend came back into the picture and our relationship died a grisly death. I enjoyed her company so much that when she dropped me like a bad habit, I would have been willing to do some serious soul selling to any half-baked demon to keep the relationship going.

Also I hate it when people spend their entire day in a pissed off or bitchy mood, but I get ahead of myself; quality number five will belabor this point rather thoroughly. If I can always find a way to make my mate laugh, and she can do the same for me, we will have a great way to pull each other out of the doldrums when the negative emotions in life inevitably rear their ugly heads. Tension relief in sticky situations, negotiating a successful path through a gathering with the in-laws, and poking fun at life's trivial problems are all good opportunities for a sense of humor to improve upon your day-to-day life. If you can add humor at the right times, your relationship will be cooler than Nanook of the North's underwear. As the guy with the collar says on the wedding day "...do you take this woman in good times and in bad...." A compatible sense of humor is certainly a great way to cut down on the aforementioned "bad."

The moral of the story is—when you are laughing, you're happy. We all want to be happy for as much of our lives as possible. The more you can find to laugh about, the more you'll enjoy being with someone and the more you will enjoy life. Simple, yet very important.

3. Self-confidence

This one is a bit more difficult to define in "perfect mate" terms, but I'll give it the old-college try anyway. The best way to describe what I'm looking for in this regard is to show you some instances where self-confidence is lacking. Example 1: the woman who relies on her mate to tell her how to do everything just short of putting the toilet seat down. Example 2: The woman who is scared to death of attempting anything new because her fear of failure outweighs her desire to experience something different.

I want someone who will be more than a faithful servant waiting on my every whim. My mate will be someone who's not afraid to strike out on her own with individual goals and ideas for a better life. Someone who will be confident enough in herself to stand with me as an equal partner and share equal responsibility in the relationship is what I want. The cave man days are over; you can't just drag them around by their hair anymore. Having a person who lives only to please you in a selfless manner, though gratifying in the short-term, gets boring-*quickly!* I need someone who has confidence in herself, who won't be afraid to question me when I'm wrong, and who will help me strive to be a better person.

This self-confidence spills over into other aspects of her life and will help make her more successful in whatever she attempts. Throw in high self-esteem to the recipe and Ms. Perfect's compatibility rating with me starts to skyrocket. After all, it has been said that I'm one notch below cocky on the self-confidence scale, and it would be nice to have her in the same ball park.

4. Intelligent

I could take two tracks of thinking on this one. 1) A woman that has little insight into her own actions and the situations around her would not stimulate me intellectually, thereby making her inherently incompatible with me. Or, 2) I'm a high-brow snob when it comes to people who choose ignorance as a way of life.

Being college educated, I would like my mate to be the same. A commonality in this regard usually breeds similar lifestyles, experiences, and attitudes. Furthermore, I want someone who I can learn from, not someone whose views for the week come from the 4 to 5 p.m. trash TV time slot. This person should help me learn how to better myself, and be able to do the same for herself.

Time is one of my most precious commodities, and I don't want to spend it getting my wife up to speed on everything happening around her. I've also noticed (a rash generalization is coming up here) that less intelligent people base many of their ideas and beliefs on emotion instead of rooting them in logic. When you challenge these beliefs, it's like running face first into a cement truck. Instead of listening and attempting to understand your point of view, they cling to their beliefs and throw argumentative gibberish back in your face. I do know some people of high intellectual capacity who can be just as guilty of zero rationale syndrome, so I know that this emotional way of life can't be universally applied to intelligence. Most of the time, however, this does seem to be the case. If my mate can comprehend what and why I do things, our communication channels will be better, and we'll have an easier trip down life's highway.

5. Lack of daily PMS bouts

Holy pet peeve Batman! This has always been a major sticking point with me. If a woman wants a quick and easy way to make sure that I'm never in the same hemisphere with her, she simply needs to get herself a case of terminal bitchiness and it will do the trick instantly. I've trashed friendships, avoided family gatherings, and quit menial jobs for just this reason.

I can't justify outward displays of unbridled anger or rage in any situation. Some people say that knock-down-drag-out fighting has many constructive effects on a relationship. It allows both people to air their differences and show their true feelings for each other and not hold anything back. Then, the story goes, that "the kiss and make-up" part of the fight makes everything in the relationship fresh again, and the sex after such a fight is downright incredible.

What a pile of crap! Screaming, punching, and yelling are just excuses for people who can't handle the pressures and responsibilities of a close relationship. It also shows an inability to communicate problems without resorting to Cro-Magnon techniques. I've seen many people who treat others with kindness and respect, but use their mate as a whipping post for their personal problems and failures. They do this because subconsciously they think "she loves me so much that I can get away with it, and she'll always forgive me." Unfortunately, this is the case too often, and it serves to perpetuate the acceptance of this ridiculous and unnecessary behavior.

Why? Why can't we deal rationally with these problems and work through them constructively instead of beating each other up emotionally and sometimes physically? People tend to treat small problems like fixing a leaky faucet with a piece of bubble gum. Instead of addressing the problem when the flow was a mere trickle, they wait until the water is squirting 10 feet high. Why not deal with the little problems as they come along? It is more difficult, requires better communication channels between the partners, and can be more time consuming, but in the grand scheme of things, it is well worth it to avoid the emotional scars that result from having knock-down-drag-out brawls.

If a woman doesn't handle life's problems in a constructive manner, she's not going to be dating me very long. This is something that I just don't understand. Have you noticed that I feel very strongly about this? I had a girlfriend in grad school who, for no real reason, blew up at me in the hallway after a class that we had together. When she came to apologize to me the next day, it fell on deaf ears. The damage was done. Before she left, I informed her of why we were history and gave her a small piece of mind by detailing how she could better control her anger in the future. It probably didn't change her one iota, but if it did, then maybe I did a minuscule part to improve her future relationships.

Why is this such a concern of mine? I've seen too many relationships destroyed when one or both people could not constructively handle their negative emotions. I can do it, the people close to me can do it, so my mate will certainly be able to do it.

The negative emotions that I'm talking about aren't necessarily just the yelling and screaming type of brawl. It may be little things like snapping at each other over petty differences. It may be a general bitchy mood one day a week. However it manifests itself, it's a waste of some precious time that I have on this planet, and we all have only a limited quantity of this. All the money in the world can't buy us extra sand in the hourglass of life, so why not make those we have as good as possible. Negative emotions also serve to bring your mate down. If you can't work through your problems, either alone or with another person, your emotions are eventually going to affect your partner. Even the happiest person will start to enjoy life less if he is constantly around a partner who doesn't enjoy their own life. Eventually, this will take its toll on the relationship. I want someone who can recognize what the cause of her problems are, work through them, and get back to her life. In doing so, we will enjoy each other's company that much more, and life will be downright copacetic.

6. Romantic

I admit it, I'm schmaltzy. When I'm falling for someone I pull out all of the stops. Flowers, candlelight dinners prepared in my very own kitchen, lying in front of the fireplace and staring into each other's glassy eyes, late night walks along the beach— I like them all and anything that even remotely resembles romance. I'm not afraid to show a woman that I care for her, and those that I've dated in the past appreciate the break from the six-pack and a night-in-front-of-the-tube type male.

I'm also very touchy-feely. Holding hands, back massages, and other PDA's (Public Displays of Affection) are some of the most called plays in my romance playbook. It makes me feel closer to the person and enhances the other parts of the relationship. At the end of a romantic evening, I get a feeling of contentment that few other things in life can provide. That's when I fall asleep in her arms or go hours without a single thought entering my mind. It's a different concept from sex, but it's a very satisfying one. Put a great sexual experience on top of a romantic evening and you find out why people throw away all sense of reality and common sense when they fall in love.

As long as I'm on the subject, sex with a romantic person is usually much better than getting horizontal with a person who's idea of romance is a horror movie and a bottle of Jack Daniel's. Romantic people are not afraid to take some time enjoying the act, to caress for a while before the big finish, and are usually more orgasmic once they get there. For any females who may be reading, that is an important insight into the male psyche. Guys do actually like romance. If a woman takes the time to plan a quiet, romantic evening, most men will appreciate and thoroughly enjoy it.

Another thing that really warms the cockles of the heart, is when I see two people well past the social security age holding hands or otherwise cavorting in public. I say to myself, "If I can be like that at their age, then I would have the world sitting right in the palms of my hands." That is definitely a sight that could tug on the heart strings of even the most stone-hearted person alive.

7. Enjoys sex

You were probably figuring that this had to be on the list somewhere. All right, let's be honest here. Sex is a part of the big package like anything else. Procreation, intimacy, and that incredible feeling you get at climax—none of these things can be attained without it.

I'm a very sexual person. I, like most males who admit it or not, have had an orgasm at least once a week since the mid-teens. I've found from my experiences that I much prefer the partnered version to the manual style. Therefore, given the twice-a-week average over the course of a 50-year marriage, I'd like my spouse to enjoy the act we'll be doing at least 6,000 times.

I've found in my travels, that a girl who enjoys sex usually takes the time to learn how to do it in a mutually satisfying manner. This, of course, increases my pleasure in the experience, and creates another one of those valuable "bringing joy to the life of your spouse" situations that I've been discussing with an overused regularity in this chapter. As another tip for any women out there, guys like women who get into sex. If you just lay there like a dead fish, the average man will be thinking of dipping his pole into another pond really quick. But if you enjoy sex, it will make the concept of being a one-fishing-hole man a lot easier to handle. Being that this is the 90s, and this topic is highly in vogue, I'll hold off on giving any more details, and devote a whole chapter to sex later.

8. Similar lifestyle and attitudes

A perfect example of this was demonstrated to me by a close friend of mine and his wife. Like many couples who got married right out of college, they found that their daily activities and hobbies were like "Frankenstein Meets the Little Mermaid." As time passed she began to develop an interest in his hobbies, and his attitudes started to become more like hers. Here is a good marriage at work. It really struck me when she entered tennis tournaments and invested hundreds of dollars in ski equipment—two of his favorite activities. At the same time his personality changed for the better as her calming and congenial traits rubbed off on him. These personality alterations were less obvious, yet they were very important because making changes in your personality is a difficult thing for anyone to accomplish.

Marriage involves a lot of give and take. In order to reap the rewards that it can give, you have to be willing to make some sacrifices. You also have to be willing to change some things about yourself to help the relationship succeed over the long-haul. This is a quality that I would like Ms. Perfect to possess. We should be similar enough in lifestyle and attitudes that if I want her to take up tennis so that we can spend time together, she will be willing to do so. And if she wants me to snip a couple of the rough edges from my life's pattern, I may kick and bite a little, but I'd be willing to do so.

9. *Ability to get along with friends and family*

If you knew my friends and family, you would know why this is on the list. Saying that my friends and relatives are a little unusual is like saying that drinking a quart of Drano might make your stomach feel queasy. In fact, if a woman can get along with both my friends and family, she's not only eligible to be my wife, but the people with the white jackets and padded walls will be beating down her door and Charles Manson will definitely want an autographed 8 x 10 glossy of her.

They say that when you marry someone that you also marry their friends. This is very important to me since my friends play a major part in my life. I don't want my wife to be jealous of one of my female friends, or not let me go party with the boys because she thinks that they'll try to get me to play the field when I'm out.

I've noticed that the closeness of my friendships have been affected by my friends' wives. This additional burden will be lightened if Ms. Perfect gets along well with my friends. As more and more people pair up, I've found that friendships are made better or worse depending upon how you and your mate get along with your friend's partner. I've seen great wives make spending time with friends more enjoyable, but I've also seen it go to the point where no matter how much you enjoy a friend's company, the wife can put a damper on the whole deal. Major gist in one line: if she's fun to be around, then everyone has more fun. If she can act just as weird and idiotic as us and fit into our group, then she's got my vote for Wife of the Year.

10. *Compassionate with kids*

Assuming here that my future wife is going to push out a couple of puppies at some point after matrimony, I want the mother of my children to be able to deal with anything from multi-colored diaper deposits to the dilemma of a 14-year-old daughter informing Mom that she wants to go on the pill and start sleeping over at Jason's house on a trial basis. If we pump out two rug rats, she has to be able to handle three kids (of course I count as one) being obnoxious, throwing tantrums, and trying to come up with the most disgusting bodily function possible just to attract attention. Of course she must do all of this without becoming psycho-woman from hell, throwing plates, screaming, or having gooey green stuff oozing out of her ears.

Tall order? Yes. But I think that someone who is stable enough to put up with me for a lifetime will have the perseverance to do the same with Satan's offspring. Just to make sure though, maybe I'll offer our baby-sitting services to my sister's four kids for a weekend before slipping the engagement ring on the finger of any prospective mate.

11. Similar phase of life

There are some little things here that are not of relationship-ending importance, but that weigh into the equation. I'm a never-married, no kids, mid-twenties person. Naturally, it would be nice if the person that I ended up with was the same.

Having a relationship with a divorcée who has a kid or two is not insurmountable given love between us, but it does make things more difficult. I'm sure that someone who has been married previously doesn't want to go through all of the grandiose plans and activities for the wedding day like someone who is on their first time. I want my wedding to be the greatest 24 hours of my life. And I would like to start my family from scratch and not have the baggage of an ex-husband and a step-father moniker hanging over my head. A child also puts limitations on the relationship in its beginning stages. We would have to do things that include the child, and our time alone to get to know each other would be limited. Also, I'm only a couple of years into being responsible for myself, much less being a positive role model for a young impressionable mind.

The age of a potential partner factors into the equation, too. Someone who is much older than I am has different life experiences and a different income expectation than someone like myself who is still a couple years out of college and is feeling the effects loanwise. If she's hitting menopause when I finally get the nerve and stability in life to consider children, this would put a big restriction on the notion of starting a family.

Again, these problems aren't insurmountable, but they are realistic issues to consider when entering into a new relationship. It's back to that sameness motif that has weaved its way throughout this chapter. If she is at the same juncture of life as I am, it makes it easier for us to progress through life together at the same pace.

12. All those little things that you remember Mom doing

Remember all the fond memories of the things that Mom did that made you think that she was the greatest person in the world? When I dropped the ball that cost my team the baseball game, there would be chocolate chip cookies waiting. The chicken soup was always piping hot when she spoonfed me on the days that I was too sick to go to school. And a hug and a kiss from Mom would make even the most painful laceration feel better.

I guess this is just a sentimental quality that I felt after getting misty when thinking back on my childhood days. It just seems that Mom always knew what to do in any situation (and when she didn't we gave her the benefit of the doubt). If my fellow siblings and I were simultaneously throwing dinner around the room, screaming, crayoning the wallpaper, and using a meat cleaver to cut my younger brother's hair, she knew how to deal with it without turning into a psychotic killer. I only hope that my wife will be able to do the same things with me and our kids.

That brings us to the end of a serious, but, nonetheless, important chapter of the book. If, by any chance you know a person who possesses all of the qualities I have just described, please send me her name, address, phone number, picture, and favorite Bugs Bunny episode. If indeed she turns out to be the woman of my dreams, then I will be forever in your debt, you will be on my Christmas card list, and we will name our first four kids after you.

This is the woman that I'm looking for to enter my life. I'm willing to settle down, but I'm not willing to settle. A good woman could possibly be the only thing on all of the seven continents that could turn me into a politically correct individual. Though I enjoy my current state of existence, I'm ready to move on. I'm ready to face the challenges of caring for someone else almost as much as I care for myself, waiting for someone who could give me a reason to aspire to a higher plane, and longing for someone to sleep next to every night. Here I am, bring her on.

Well Then, Where the Hell is She?

Where to Look for the Perfect Woman

Big deal. I know what I'm looking for. What good has that done me so far in this lifetime? Why hasn't some genie popped out of a magic lamp, put my ideal woman in front of me, with her first words being "If you've got lots of soap, I'll wash you from head-to-toe for two straight weeks!" I love women, I brush regularly, and I don't pick my nose in public, so how come in 26 years I haven't found anyone who even remotely resembles my ideal woman? My friends have wives that I'd be happy to take home to Mom, but I've only met the Charlie Brown Christmas trees of the dating world.

Okay. Maybe my approach is wrong. Could it be that spending two nights a week at the local taverns looking only to do the horizontal bop with someone isn't helping me to attain my goal? I'm still holding out for the one-in-a-million shot that the right one is only a beer away at a local establishment. I must admit my feelings about this method have changed. I used to believe that I would never meet my fantasy woman in a bar, but of late my hook-up skills are better than the average bar flunky. I have perfected the art of the bar pick-up to the point that I give the appearance of being someone that a great woman could be interested in. In fact, I'll go so far as to say that I may be able to find the woman of Chapter 2 in a bar if I look to find her rather than thinking from my groin every night. I hereby resolve to spend my weekly bar time searching for a woman worth spending more than a night with. This will require a few minor alterations to my pick-up process. However, I've reached the point where I'm able to resist the temptation of searching for immediate satisfaction instead of pursuing someone who could provide it for the long term.

My rules, regulations, and methodologies for the bar pick-up of a dateable woman are as follows. The most important thing to know when perusing the available female choices is who wants to be picked-up and who would rather run you through with a pitchfork than talk. It's usually as simple as a pleasant look on her face versus the woman whose face says, "Talk to me and I'll remove at least four of your vital organs." If she's looking around at the crowd, that's a good sign. If a girl doesn't want to meet someone you're wasting valuable bar time that could be spent with another prospect who could give you the time of day and potentially much more. Also important here is to make sure that her looks are up to snuff before you even make your approach. Think to yourself, could I wake up next to that for the next 50 years, or would grabbing a nearby athletic bag and saying, "I'm off to baseball practice, lock up when you leave," be your first action upon waking up with her on the morning after? If you chose the latter, then move on to the next one.

After you find someone who appears to be approachable, the next step is to do the all important "ring check" on the third finger of the left hand. An affirmative on the ring check is like seeing the closed sign in the window of a store—married women are obviously a waste of time unless you're a practicing Mormon.

Now comes the big opening line. Scrap the corn ball stuff. It can work on occasion, but sticking to the basics is much more successful. I had one friend who, while carousing in a drunken stupor, went behind a girl, lifted her off the ground then set her back down. He then told her "Now I can say that I've picked-up the best looking girl in the bar." Amazingly enough it worked and he took her home that night. She must have felt sorry for him that he was desperate enough to have to use a line like that. Maybe she just had the brain capacity of a lug wrench. You make the call.

As an aside, I'll give you a couple of lines of a more sexual nature that have been favorites among some of my friends. 1) "I couldn't help but notice that you have a size 7 crotch and I have a size 7 face—I think we've got something here!" 2) Along the same line yet simpler—"As long as I'm alive, you've got a place to sit." These lines will probably never get you anything except a slap in the face, but we have been told that all men are perverts enough times in our lives, so why not keep the stereotype going?

The only slightly corny one that I use on occasion is "I'm sorry, you're not meeting your minimum enthusiasm quota. You'll either have to look much happier or leave the bar immediately." It almost always gets a laugh and your foot in the door at the same time. Next do the standard where are you from, what do you do for a living stuff. The important thing is to show a genuine interest in what she does. Ask her a couple of questions about her job and find out what she likes and doesn't like about it. It will show that you care about something besides your almighty self and will make her feel more comfortable talking to you. Remember, everyone on this planet enjoys talking about himself or herself more than anything else. Making a joke about something positive about her will give you some big bonus points. Important safety tip here—avoid making any comments that rip on her profession. Even if she stuffs envelopes for 40 hours each week, make her feel like you would need six years of schooling to be successful at her job. All in all, make her feel good about herself— that's the key. Everyone wants to feel good about himself or herself, and if you do that for her, you'll be much more attractive in her eyes. By all means never utter the phrase "Isn't that a man's job?" unless you have a stopwatch handy to see how quick- ly the phrase "I've gotta go find my friends, see you later" can be uttered by a pissed off female.

I've noticed that the pick-up process is very similar to a salesman's pitch, the only difference being that the product that you are selling is yourself. After your opening statement, the next step is the presentation of your product. This is the most impor- tant part of the sales process. Always keep in tune to what she's saying and add a dash of flattery—it works like a charm. It's like putting on cologne—a couple a dabs here and there is great, but over use it and you will reek of an unpleasant aroma. Bullshit, that is, country style. Making references to things she said earlier in the conversation is another great technique. This is especially true if she says something that you find to be particularly funny. Bringing it up in a different way later in the conversation shows that not only do you care about the things she's saying, but that you thought about it enough to ship it off to long-term memory.

Now look for the little signals. These are your best gauge as to what your likely success rate will be. Is she laughing a lot at what you say? Is she looking around for any excuse to say "Beat it reject?" Is her comfort space between the two of you get- ting closer or is she still talking to you from somewhere in Indiana? All of these things, plus the other little signs like touches, slapping you on the shoulder if you jok- ingly make fun of her, and solid eye contact, will help you to find out if you'll get a chance with her or if your date for tonight will be your palm and a few fingers.

Going to bars with a dance floor gives you another great pick-up tool in the slow dance. Even if you only possess the rhythm of a picnic table you can still dance to slow songs and look like you know what you're doing. Just grab on, get close, turn to the right every now and then, and you'll look like Denny Terio in no time. There are some important things to notice here, too. Is she looking around at everyone else to avoid having to see you up close and personal? Would a yard stick fit in between the two of you with plenty of room to spare? When you try to pull her close does she start discussing her recipe for broccoli quiche? All these things are like neon signs flashing "No Vacancy" in your general direction.

There are some good signs, too. Anytime she initiates closing the gap between the two of you is a definite plus. Hands rubbing up and down on your back shows definite interest. Then there is my favorite. When the dance ends, if she gives you a tight hug and lets out a trembling noise almost like she just came out of a blizzard with nothing on but slinky underwear, take her home right now, because she wants you in a big way.

Be a bit leery if she's too friendly at this point. If your pants catch on fire due to the friction caused by her rubbing your crotch with hers, chances are that she's been around the block more times than the ice cream truck. Take her home tonight for some bed squeaking, but seriously question her ability to be monogamous for longer than an average feature length film.

Unlike what we males with a sleazy past are normally accustomed to, the object of the first night isn't getting horizontal; it's getting her phone number, a kiss, and a date commitment. Make sure to tell her your plans for the first date before you say good-bye. This will help to build the anticipation in her mind until she sees you again. Of course, in order to create this mental excitement you have to come up with a plan that she'll look forward to. Don't be afraid to try something different. Wine tasting tours are always my favorite. It shows creativity above the standard dinner and a movie, and when you get a bunch of fermented grapes in a woman you'll both have a better time. If you don't live in New York, California, or one of the handful of other wine producing states (or if you're just not into wine tasting), you will have to come up with a memorable first date idea. Be original, and remember that a drive of 200 miles to see something like the U.S. Buffalo Chip Throwing Championships isn't a major turn-on for the average woman. Timing is important here too. If it's Friday or Saturday when you meet her, try to set something up for the next day, or at least within the next couple of days. How much more she enjoyed your company versus the other 50 guys who hit on her in the last week fades very quickly.

One time I met a girl on Friday and set plans for a date with her on Sunday. It just happened that Saturday her old boyfriend called, and begged her to take him back. By the time that I called her on Sunday she was back together with him, had probably consecrated the rebirth of the relationship once or twice, and wanted to see me as much as she wanted colon cancer.

Another important tip about setting up that first date is the increasingly popular trend with the female gender to give you their work number instead of the home version. This doesn't mean that you're in the archives even before getting out of the starting blocks. A lot of women are becoming more cautious in this day and age and figure that their secretary is already a professional in making up excuses why they can't come to the phone. That way if you turn out to be some psycho from hell, they can just have the secretary add you to the list of people who hear the phrase "Sorry, she's in a meeting right now." Translation: Right buddy, you'll talk to her when pigs fly out my butt. So don't be taken aback if she ends the date by giving you the work number.

That's the bar process in its simplest version. It hasn't helped me to find my ideal woman yet, but it has gotten me a lot of dates that had spouse potential. Slight alteration of the formula has also gotten me a lot of sex. But now that I've taken on this newfound relationship frame of mind, I'm not seeking the one night sex endeavors anymore. I'm shedding my male instincts and I'm looking for someone for life. But of course, should some wanton woman throw herself into my arms and say "Ride me, you sexual cowboy," I won't look a gift horse in the mouth. Old habits die hard you know. I am still realistic.

I have also vowed to expand my search for other places where I could find this fantasy woman. I've already blown the number one opportunity to find a woman by not staying sober enough to land one during my college years. I would bet that one out of four people who go to college end up finding their spouse there. It makes sense though. What other time in your adult life are you surrounded by so many people of similar backgrounds, age and life experiences? You are free to meet these people in an environment that has no rules, supervision, and limited responsibilities. That certainly makes the process a lot easier.

The type of college that you go to even helps you to get someone of your same socio-economic group and similar career track. A word to anyone out there who is reading this while attending college. Start shopping around now because the shelves of the mate supermarket start to look more and more like those of the Moscow Shop & Save the older you get.

Let's look to something else and try to identify some different approaches to locate the perfect woman. How about the proverbial party circuit. Back in my days of wild raging hormones and almost legal drinking age, me and the boys used to whip one up every week that was like dipping a line in at the fish hatchery. You were guaranteed to land something. The only difference here from normal fishing was that in this case you hoped that the "big one" did get away and didn't end up in your bed. As I've gotten older and more of my friends are married, we have mostly the same group of people attending our gatherings and I receive fewer invites to shindigs hosted by other people.

Parties are good, though, because as I've said earlier, you're looked at as a friend versus being a stranger. I have one friend who was so good at the party pick-up that he had classifications for the ways to do it. As a party pro, he knew how to be the center of attention, how to find the girl who liked guys who were the hit of the party, how to play the sensitive guy and attract a woman by showing compassion in a sea of sex-starved partyers, or even a fake alcohol-enhanced depression to lure a compassionate woman into his trap. Besides the numerous sex encounters he actually got some good relationships out of it.

The problem I've had a couple of times though, is that when you put on the party attitude and become the life of the party you can attract someone who only digs your party persona. A couple of dates later when you discover that you could actually invite her to a family gathering or do something with her that has a bit of the "commitment" word attached to it, she pulls a disappearing act rivaling anything Houdini could have ever put together.

The reasons for this are two-fold. First, she thought you were just a fun-loving guy who could provide her with some good times without any strings attached. It's the classic "good girls who like bad boys" situation. She just wants to hang out for a couple nights, spend some fun times and then fade off into the sunset. It's a mutual usury not meant to have any permanent feelings involved, just a lot of laughs and some good times. Basically it is the same thing that a lot of guys do regularly with women, but our male egos are crushed when it happens to us.

Second, even if she does have thoughts of something with more substance to it, many guys become plagued with Getting Serious Syndrome. When this happened to me with a "met-her-at-a-party-had-some-fun" woman I pulled a complete about face, and showed her the serious, or even worse, the sensitive side of my personality. Of course, when the commitment signs started flashing my devil-may-care attitude slipped and her boredom with me went up faster than the Space Shuttle. This side of my personality wasn't as wild, which was the main thing she enjoyed about me in the first place. Also, instead of seeing just another woman that I discovered at a party, when I looked into those eyes of hers, I saw more than the opportunity for another sexual encounter. I saw Relationship SuperWoman. More powerful than my VISA card speeding quickly to its credit limit, able to make me leap over lifelong friends when she wanted me to Simonize her car, faster than the 100 mph that my vehicle goes when she ran her hand up my leg while I was driving. This woman was on a pedestal higher than Mt. Everest. She was the one that I wanted to fulfill all of my schmaltziest desires with, but she didn't want anything to do with me anymore. She wanted the hard-core partier that she met during a drink-until-you-puke party game. The new me repelled her like a negatively charged electromagnet.

I would like to think that I have learned from these past debacles and that women I meet at the parties of today would like to spend time with someone who is more than Mr. Nonstop Partyman. Who knows? At any rate, parties are always a good option for finding Ms. Dreamgirl. Besides, you should never turn down an opportunity for a good party.

There is an even better brand of party for meeting Ms. Right. It is a special day-long occasion that some Mr. and Mrs. call their wedding day. A bunch of guys and girls who don't know each other get dressed up, gather up their friends and family, and do lots of silly things for the sake of love and tradition. It's a huge party and every unmarried person there thinks about what it would be like to be in the shoes of the bride or groom. Normally a party of this caliber is a great environment to hook-up, but, taken one step further, if you happen to be in the wedding (i.e., a tux-clad individual) the opportunity is unparalleled. Donning formal wear at a wedding is an open opportunity to talk to every female in the place without hesitancy or restrictions. It is an invitation to request dances, toasts, and conversation in the name of making the day more special for the bride and groom. Basically it's free reign to find the best available woman, and take your best shot. Sitting at the head table and being a part of the show you are like the prime-choice meats that people peer at through the glass at the supermarket deli counter. A friend announcing his engagement is a better person to suck-up to than both your boss and an arresting officer.

Buy him drinks, send birthday cards to his parents, cart his ugly younger sister back and forth to soccer practice if you have to. Just get yourself a seat behind that head table. This way you ensure yourself the opportunity to be in the middle of a stream ripe with marriageable fish, to cast your line in waters where the game you seek want more than anything to be caught.

No chapter on finding a mate would be complete without mentioning the universal institution of the "blind date." This time-honored tradition occurs when one's friends/relatives believe you to be so incredibly desperate that you would actually be attracted to one of their equally desperate pals/relations. Depending on the judgement, taste, and degree of sadistic tendencies of the fixer-upper, this can range anywhere from a good opportunity with someone that you share commonalties with, to a night of unending, living hell.

Unfortunately, in the long-run, both the good and bad outcomes are usually losing battles for you and the other blind date guinea pig. If, by chance, you should be initially attracted to her, you must constantly be overseen by the friend/relative who made your newfound link-up possible. This way they will be able to monitor, mediate, and meddle with your relationship without discretion. They will view your personal life with an interest like never before, because you are now their pet project that temporarily helps them forget about their ordinarily mundane existence. Though they will stop at nothing to make things work between you and Ms. Datewoman, instead they will end up royally screwing up the whole deal sooner or later. Also they will subject you to a constant barrage of nauseating phrases like "They're my cute little couple" and "Aren't they great together—I did that" whenever you are in the same vicinity as them. This alone can be enough to make the prospect of a blind date very unattractive.

Of course, the other scenario of not getting along can be even more excruciating. In this case, for the six or seven months following the "disaster date," you get the constant questions of "Why didn't it work out?" drilled into you—the equivalent of a simultaneous root canal in every tooth. Back in my young and sexually naive days, before I knew the socially accepted physical limitations for each date during the beginning phases of a relationship, I once made the mistake of being too aggressive on the first outing with a friend's sister. Because she thought that I only wanted her for sex her interest in me quickly died. I moved on, she had no hard feelings, and the world was still the same place as it was the night before. However, my friend now had a piece of ammunition in his arsenal similar to a nuclear warhead, and my only defense had the equivalent power of a rolled up newspaper. For months he was relentless in abusing me about the situation (like all truly good friends are), and to this day I get the occasional jab about this ancient happening. At least two things did result from the experience: 1) I will not even attempt to do anything that could even be construed as "light petting" on the first date with a friend, relative, or enemy of someone that I know; and 2) I won't have to worry about rule #1 because I will never go out with someone in that category again until the day before I die or until Elvis leaves his job at the 7-Eleven in Kalamazoo, Michigan, to produce five more gold records, whichever comes first.

What about some other dating ideas? I could find my dream woman by doing some volunteer work. The women involved here would definitely be more caring and compassionate than the average female. It's a good friendly environment to meet people, and I'd even get a bonus. I would feel good because I'd be giving back something to the society that I'm usually taking from. Something like the Big Brother/Big Sister program might work. Even better, working with kids at a local hospital would be a less expensive way to meet nurses than a self-induced major illness. I've dated a couple of nurses that were definitely good prospects. They're usually more caring than the average person with two X chromosomes, intelligent, and their knowledge of anatomy and lack of fear of exploring it can be big pluses. Maybe I should "manufacture" some kind of physical accident that is relatively minor in the long run, but will require a long stay in the hospital and daily sponge baths from a voluptuous blonde dressed in white. Maybe a broken hip would be enough to land me a nurse to take home for life. O.K., I'm losing my precious grip on reality here. Let's get back to the real world. We'll now return you to our regularly scheduled dating guide.

How about this? Have you ever heard of the Laundromat routine? Pretend to be incapable of figuring out the difficult concepts of detergent, fabric softener and bleach, only to have your dream woman rescue you and begin the trip to the land of happily ever after. If you've never done it don't even waste the thought to consider it. Except for the laundromat that doubles as a bar in the beer commercials, no female that could fit in jeans under size 12 or has a full set of molars frequents a laundromat. Also, what kind of economic background does someone have if they don't own or have access to a washer and dryer? Third, if they think that you are too stupid to read the back of a cardboard box, then I'd question whether they passed the fourth grade themselves. Maybe the laundromats in your area are different, but believe me, in my college days when I lived in places without the modern convenience of free laundry, my experiences with laundromats were exactly as stated above. By the way, if you still plan to disregard my recommendation to stay away from the launderama as a method of meeting women, make sure to deck yourself out in polyester from head to toe. The women at these fine establishments will be digging your scene much more that way.

Next option: people that you work with. The viability of this obviously depends upon the nature of your work, the size of the company, and how many unmarried women are in your office. For those working at the Fortune 500 companies of our fine country I'm sure those company Christmas parties are a veritable breeding ground for an inter-office romance. On the other hand I'm sure that the average sanitation worker may have a bit of difficulty finding that someone special at the workplace.

The acceptability of said relationships also varies depending upon the corporate culture at your work place. At one company I worked for, if the boss found out that his secretary was having a sexual, extra-curricular relationship with another employee, she got canned immediately, and the guy got a harsh reprimand. His response to this type of thing was a bit harsh and somewhat illegal, but his mindset was that his secretary knew some important things that an unscrupulous person with any persuasion power over her could use to the disadvantage of the company. That could cost him a lot of money. That doesn't make what he did right, but I can understand where he's coming from.

The anticipated post-relationship animosity between two co-workers can also hinder the desire to start such an endeavor. Any good boss can sense both love and hate vibes between two people, and he/she may hold your inability to function with your former lover/co-worker against you come the corporate-ladder-climbing time. A rule of thumb here would be to stay away from officemates, your secretary, your boss, or any one you see on a daily basis. Going for someone like the girl in accounting who you pass in the office twice a year, occasionally eye from across the cafeteria at lunch, and who would provide a downright solid second income should things develop—that would be acceptable and also feasible. It all depends upon your specific work situation. Just make sure to consider all of the ramifications before entering into an inter-office romance.

Then there are the various social clubs. Of these, ski clubs are usually one of the biggest (provided you are north of the Mason-Dixon). These are interesting and have potential. Although most people in these clubs do indeed ski, you don't have to be a skier to participate because they are basically year round singles clubs that use skiing as a guiding theme.

I went to a meeting for one when I was in college. I saw a pretty even mixture of people in their low 20's to mid 40's. Not many would have passed my physical appearance standards for the ideal mate, but this type of club could lend itself to some serious partying, fun skiing, and even an occasional broken bone. I've been thinking about checking out one of the local ones, but I haven't gotten around to it yet. I'll keep it in mind for later.

Other types of clubs are good options because you will most likely have common interests with female club members that you can use as a starting block to interact with them. Clubs also provide you with a non-threatening environment in which to meet people, and you get to share activities with them that you both enjoy. All of these things are big pluses.

One of the last choices of places to find a prospective mate, which exists in large and small towns everywhere, is the dreaded personal ads. I haven't sunk to this level yet. There is a certain stigma about them that makes you think, "If I'm so desperate that I need to respond to a personal ad, I must be a real loser." I don't know if I can trust the descriptions that people give about themselves. Don't you think that the phrase "petite" could range in translation from fit-and-trim to, "Doritos are my life?" What are the phrases "full-figured, and nicely proportioned" trying to hide? How about this one that I recently saw during a flip through the personal pages, "My name is Rose, I'm 24, honest, secure, attractive, and looking for a man to have a good time with." Well, a girl's got to have her standards. As long as you have a pulse and a penis you're not going to disappoint old Rose. I'll hold off on this method for a while. Maybe you'll see me on Love Connection next season. But then again, maybe not.

The next option, which is one step further up the serious-steps-to-dating ladder both in a monetary sense and in commitment, is a dating service. I mean the legal ones here, not "escort services," or whatever the current terminology for organized prostitution is these days. The legal ones start at least $100 for each of the people involved. There are some advantages here, though. You find out in advance appearance, background and interests of the person before signing on the dating dotted line. So, it's not like a blind date with Aunt Irma's hairdresser's daughter's friend, Michelle, who according to all reports from Irma, her hairdresser, and her daughter, is a "fantastic girl." The cost of using a dating service also imposes an unwritten financial restriction upon the people who use them. If someone is willing to shell out 100 bucks just to have the opportunity to meet someone, chances are that they are financially stable and serious about finding a significant other. This dating service thing definitely has potential.

Well there you have it. That's my list of prospective places to find Ms. Perfect. There may be some that I forgot or that I gave a bad rap to because of personal experiences, but the bottom line is—anywhere that you see potential, give it a try. Personally, I've probably limited myself because I haven't tried the ideas that are outside my ordinary realm of activities. I'm not afraid to join a ski club or contact a dating service, and they are not cost prohibitive for me. I simply haven't given them much consideration until now. These ways of finding a woman are different, sometimes expensive, and have never been needed by any of my married friends. Whereas going to bars, although dealing with a low success rate in finding dateable people, is easy, fun, and if I don't find someone to love, I can usually find someone to move the stick shift of my sexual transmission into the "drive" position.

Now that I think about it, maybe I am hindering my cause by not placing a priority on doing things and going to places where I stand a better chance of hooking up with the ideal mate. Maybe I'll make it a late New Year's Resolution to get out of my normal pattern of life and take some actions that will put me on this path. That makes two changes that I've promised myself in three chapters. Maybe this finding a wife thing is starting to have a newfound importance in my life. It's all just a matter of what's important to you and what course you want to take in life. I guess I've talked myself into it, though—dating service here I come!

Playing the Dating Game

The First Date Agenda

Well folks—it finally happened. Through a fine-tuned balance of luck, charm, and wit, I have actually met someone who I am interested in having a relationship with. There I was, hanging out with a couple of friends while scoping the babes at a local pub on a Friday night. After a few drinks I perused the available pickings for the evening and one girl stood out in the crowd like a well-kept mare in a group of "soon-to-be-glue" horses. I kept an eye on her until my opportunity arose, and when it did I made my strategic play. Nothing fancy. I simply introduced myself, cocky smile in tow, and asked her to dance. After that it all went exactly as planned. My bar pick-up agenda was laid out with precise detail, and it worked to a T. First we did some talking. That allowed me to find out the vitals about her. I had to make sure that she wasn't just a walking, talking, pee-her-pants, Barbie-doll type woman. Throughout the conversation, I made sure to put my best foot forward with some humorous and clever discourse, while simultaneously evaluating whether or not her pretty face came included with a fully functional personality. This continued for a couple of hours. I was enjoying her company so much that, with the exception of a couple of breaks for slow dances, we talked non-stop. We didn't even realize that the place was slowly clearing out until we noticed that we were the last two customers left in the place.

From what I could ascertain from our conversation her personality had all of the qualities I'd been searching for. She's smart, funny, self-confident, and cared very much about the people around her. Her name is Becky. Physically, she's very attractive. She has long dirty blonde hair, not the hair-spray big haired fru-fru-girl type. Her wavy locks surrounded a make-up-not-required-pretty-even-at-7 a.m. kind of face. All in all, the package was definitely a winner.

The bar owners finally asked us to leave because the janitor was sick of sweeping empty cups and other crap around us. I remember saying to myself throughout the conversation, "Pete, she's got serious potential, don't screw it up." And though I was donning my most carefree, self-confident attitude, I was almost in disbelief. Her signals made it clear that she was saying the same thing to herself.

When we walked to her car my heart was pounding as I leaned forward to give her the kiss that I was waiting for all night. After a minute or two of lip-lock, she informed me that she never had as much fun in a bar as she had that evening. She then scrolled those all important seven-digits onto a bar napkin that I had conveniently put into my pocket earlier for just that purpose. We kissed again and then parted. The smiles on both of our faces were so big that we must have looked like we had the Oscar Meyer Weinermobile lodged sideways in our mouths.

Upon waking up the next day I immediately thought of the night's events and felt that same smile burst across my face. I realized that I did something that would have made my Mom proud, versus my usual Friday night activities that would make her want to wash my mouth (and possibly some other areas) with soap. The anticipation had built all morning as I looked forward to making that big call. I occasionally looked at the bar napkin just to stare at the number for a while to make sure that the whole thing wasn't just some fantasy that my brain concocted during a 4 a.m. dream. When I finally dialed her number it felt as though my pulse was somewhere in the mid-300s.

I heard a soft voice on the other end of the phone line. Her "Hello" sounded almost musical, and it alone triggered memories of the fun I had the night before. I felt like some construction worker named Jake was operating a sledgehammer where my heart used to be. I tried to say, "Hello, this is Peter," and enough phlegm lined my windpipe to make me sound like a seventh-grade boy who was just sprouting body hair. "Settle down boy; get back to your normally cocky self. If you show fear she'll smell it on you better than Lassie ever could, and she'll send you packing in a heartbeat," I thought.

During our 10 minute conversation things flowed very smoothly. She remembered who I was, she still liked me, and she hadn't decided to become a lesbian since our meeting—all good things. I made a few safe jokes, rehashed a couple funny scenes from last night, and set up my favorite first date: the wine tasting trip. Stage I—"The Date Set-Up" was a complete success.

Next I fumbled through eight or nine wardrobe ideas, complaining to myself that I was acting like a girl, and finally chose the ensemble I'd originally selected from my closet. I got ready, jumped in the car, and drove to her apartment. All simple activities, yet the importance of the day made them seem more complicated than a ninth-grade-math-problem with two trains leaving at different speeds with X minutes until a catastrophic collision. Her apartment building was definitely up-scale. Either she never spendt a dime of her paychecks, or her teaching job must have paid well. As the door swung open I was greeted at the door by that same pretty smile that I'd left the night before, and I gave her a peck on the lips to show how happy I was to see her again.

Let the testing begin. Whether you are consciously aware of it or not, the first date is where you begin the first of hundreds of tests to see if she'll pass muster as a relationship candidate. You inspect everything about her with the thorough scrutiny of a police detective. First is the inspection of her living quarters. Would the apartment pass the white glove test? Does she have the interior-decorating gene that would allow her to make even the most drab place look like something right out of *Better Homes and Gardens*? Are there half eaten bags of potato chips laying around? This could mean that she is cellulite just waiting to happen? The skeptic here would look for pictures of a husband and kids or even a stray pair of men's underwear in the bathroom that she might have forgotten to hide. Instead, I concentrated on finding good things about her rather than searching for the bad. Not that I was going into this with blinders on, but if you place all your efforts to find the bad in people, that's what you'll find. If you look for the good your search will produce more beneficial results. Wasn't it Confucius who originally said that?

It's important to find something about her dwelling to compliment her about. Even if a nuclear bomb would be the best way to improve the appearance of the place, you should find something worthy of a genuine compliment. People are always glad to hear something nice about the place they call home. Fortunately Becky's abode would have put Felix Unger to shame in the neatness department. That was a definite check in the plus column for her.

After a few minutes of idle conversation we started on our way to Upstate New York's finest wine country. More talking, laughing, and even a few minor ventures into serious conversations covering what we wanted out of life. By then I'd filled my first-date quota by making two or three verbal miscues. When they came out I did my best to cover them up with a couple of off-the-cuff jokes about my difficulty in getting used to the mouth that I rented for this special occasion. But hey, nobody's perfect. Becky had a couple of tongue-tied moments as well, so I didn't feel so bad.

The car ride to the date site is another good testing ground for a potential relationship. In this case the trip was about an hour long—time enough to find out if there was a history of psychotic behavior in her family, for her to tell me if she couldn't handle being a man and had a sex change a few years back, or that she had a 40-foot pet anaconda named Gigi waiting for her back home. Of course these are all things that you don't inform someone about on the night that you meet them.

The car ride can also give you the opportunity to begin removing the barriers that hide your real self. This is the start of the process in which you strip off that "bar" facade and let someone get to know the part of you that harbors your emotions. For some the serious persona may be an exact replica of the social side, but for me there is an equally important facet of my personality beneath the surface. By revealing this part of myself I can find out if a woman is only interested in my social character, or if she can handle the fact that there is a intelligent, caring, and even boring side to the semi-party animal.

By allowing Becky to observe that part of me she got to find out what causes my actions, and it allowed her to see the roots of my emotions. Hopefully she'd do the same, and we'd make the climb to the second or third step on the "getting to know you" staircase. If I found out that her serious side was limited to the day she cried because every store in the mall was out of her favorite color of leather belts, we could be history faster than a "one-hit wonder" rock group. But, if there was an equally attractive person inside her outer shell, then she'd get more of those all-important relationship points, which would put her ever closer to a passing grade on the relationship test.

This is a make-or-break situation for both people. The success of the initial view into each other's personal side helps to determine if the relationship will progress further or if it will be broken off after two or three dates. If she's really unimpressed by the whole experience, then I'd probably get the token, "I had a nice time," peck on the cheek and a glimpse that said, "I hope I never see this loser again," out of the corner of her eye as she jumped out of the car.

Conversely, if I'm not interested after this it can go one of two ways. If her personality is so distasteful that I would rather ship myself off to the monastery than spend another minute with her, then she would get the "It was fun, I'll call you." Of course all men know that this phrase is a mere pleasantry because it is only uttered when a man would rather eat a seven-course meal of glass shards than speak to the woman again.

The second scenario was that her personality wasn't that bad, so I'd keep her around for a while for company and sex. In this case, the average testosterone-laden male will put up with the personality flaws for a while, knowing that eventually the relationship would end. Bad female company and sex is better than none of either. When things become less tolerable and you're looking to move on, that's when you politely let things slide. Hopefully, neither of us would end this date in any of those ways, but you never know. Most relationships die a horrible death when they are barely out of the starting gates.

After getting the serious conversation out of the way you get to the "interaction in public tests." That is where you start to make mental notes of her behavior. Do the other people that we come in contact with think she is amusing? Does she mix well with other people? Does she grab the butt of the comely male tour-guide after three sips of wine? Most of all, do we have a great time during the date, or does it go slower than an old man out for a Sunday drive on a country road? All of these things are part of that subconscious testing package that I put her through. I did this knowing that she was probably simultaneously putting me through the same mental wringer. You may not even realize that you are evaluating the other person at the time, but come the day's end you'll be able to look back at all of her actions and begin to formulate a picture of where she will fit into your future dating plans.

At this point in the date I was hoping to get some signals of affection. Would she let me hold her hand during the tour? Would she nonchalantly slide away when I tried? Or at the other extreme, when we round a corner that obstructed us from the view of others would she turn, grab me and start a deep kissing session that had an intensity much like the once a week "I thought I'd never see you again" scene in the average soap opera?

Becky did show that she was more affectionate than the average woman. After we left the winery she initiated a mini kissing session in the parking lot. She also wasn't afraid to touch me, smile at me, and display other niceties that gave me warm feelings about her. These were all checks in the plus column.

Next it was dinner time. Being the closet romantic that I am, I picked a hillside restaurant with a picturesque view that overlooked a lake. This is a perfect forum for a man who is well-schooled in the social graces to strut his stuff. Remember—white wine with chicken or fish, red with meat or pasta. Also, no matter how much you like them, never order crab legs or whole lobster on a first date. Both give you numerous opportunities to send food pieces flying across the restaurant and can make those with even the best table manners look like good King Henry at a meeting of the Knights of the Roundtable.

The conversation during dinner provides you with the proper venue to tell some of your best warm-and-fuzzy kind of stories. Women of the '90s like to see that a man has a compassionate side. Something about your grandparents that is particularly heart-warming, or even better, a story about your dog—how could that go wrong? I have a couple of touching stories about my Dad that I reserve especially for this occasion.

Aside from the negative points that a woman could accumulate if she doesn't use utensils or belches to the beat of the Frank Sinatra dinner music, the meal should be relaxing and fun just like the rest of the day. Your dinnertime discourse will help you to find out if you can still find things to say to each other after being together for five straight hours or if you find yourself drawn to the baseball game on the TV out of sheer boredom.

On my date with Becky the answer to whether she passed all of the first-date tests was a resounding "yes!" It was a very enjoyable day. Everything that I thought when I first met her had been confirmed. She was easy to talk to, very pleasant to be around, and had a warmth that everyone around her noticed. At the same time she was funny. I love when I'm with a woman who makes me laugh so hard that abdominal pain sets in. Her thoughts about today's society also showed me that the round thing above her shoulders is much more than dead weight to keep her neck muscles toned. I couldn't have asked for anything more.

The last phase of the evening was the hour car ride home. If everything went as planned there would be a portion of the ride during which we'd get caught up in a general feeling of contentment. This is a time when no words are spoken for a few minutes. We'd simply listen to the mellow tape that I made for the occasion and get caught up in the happiness that a great day with someone can provide you. If she did something like put her head on my shoulder and close her eyes, that would be a good indication that she felt the same way that I did. When Becky did that about half way through our homeward trek, I knew that we were in business!

When we got back to her apartment we became wrapped in a deep kiss even before the car engine stopped. It was a good kiss. It was a long kiss. It was a kiss that said, "This is aces. Let's do this again as soon as possible. We aren't going to call a priest today, but if this keeps going, then someday who knows." It was a kiss that showed the power of caring for another person and the amazing sensations that it brings. Hell, it was two people pressing two tongues, and four lips together for extended periods of time causing both of us to salivate and inevitably end up with this liquid deposited on or around each other's lips. But, ain't it great?

After this there is one last thing that she could do to put me over the edge. If she gives me a tight hug with a shiver at the end, that's the clincher—I've got her locked up tighter than the First National Bank of Harlem. When she did the old hug-and-shiver I knew that this could be a great thing. But I didn't want to make her feel like I was rushing things, so I talked with her for a few more minutes, shared with her that I enjoyed the day, and set up the next date. Finally, being the eternal gentleman, I walked her to her door, kissed her once more and got that Weinermobile smile again as I turned to leave. When I get back to my car I thought "This is the one. She's great in every detail. I could fall head over heels really quick."

Stop! You moron, what the hell are you thinking? Take those thoughts and throw them out of your head immediately. This is where the male brain has to take over for the idiotic heart before it blows the whole deal. If I were to call her that night, tell her what I felt and how much I enjoyed being with her, I'd be hitting the showers faster than a major league pitcher who throws underhand. It was time to do what all good men have to do in order to control themselves in a relationship—mind games. Twist things, stay on top, never let her see you sweat.

The cerebral contests of relationships really do suck, but the beginning phases of the dating process are very delicate. All it takes is one misplaced statement of your feelings, one inkling that you want to move faster than she does, and out comes the dreaded "Things are moving too fast, I think we should slow it down." Translation: "I know that I've got you wrapped around my finger. It was too easy and you bore me now. Get away from me you rutting pig." After that, things would never be what you want them to be, and if she'd ever get her head back on straight, you'd probably be old, gray, and have dentures where your teeth used to be.

This is where you have to ignore your feelings a bit for the long-term good of the relationship. First, never, ever, ever call her that night. It's like fishing. Once you have the hook stuck in the fish's mouth, you don't want to reel it in without a fight. You want to play it out a bit. You know that you will get it in the boat eventually. Why not have some fun with it? If you reel it right in and go too fast, it will be the "one that got away."

Here is a perfect example. I was talking with a girl who is a good friend of mine. She's very attractive, successful, outgoing—the all-around marrying type. She could probably have most any guy that she set her mind to. In the course of her 26 single years she's had numerous men who have all of the things that girls are supposedly looking for throw themselves at her feet. All have gone by the wayside in favor of those that end up treating her like a piece of used furniture. When I asked her why, her response was simply that the guys she turns down are too easy. Because they present no challenge to get, they get thrown away like yesterday's newspaper, or worse, get doomed to the eternal pit of the "nice guy" damnation summed up in the phrase "you're such a good friend." Instead, she goes for the ones that are a big conquest to win over. After time she gets fed up with the pathetic treatment that they give her and she dumps them, only to find herself back looking for a new mate in the wrong category.

Guys do the same thing. If she's doing your laundry, knitting you sweaters, and calling you just to say that she misses you after the first date, chances are you'll say "adios" soon after the laundry and the sweater are done.

It's all a balancing act. You have to say the right things to show that you're interested, but not be so blatant that you scare her away by coming on too strong too soon. There will be plenty of time to express how you feel in the future, so relax for now. This is part of the reason relationships are so complicated and fail much more often than they succeed. Judging someone else's expectations (and acting within their realm of acceptability) is extremely complicated to say the least. I wish it was as easy to fall in love as it is to make friendships. If I could attract my dream woman by watching football, drinking beer, telling crude jokes, and exploring the endless possibilities for amusement caused by flatulence, I'd definitely be married by now. Unfortunately for me, and many fellow males, it doesn't work that way.

Instead, I have to play the games and temper my feelings while doing the amazing high-wire balancing act that is a requirement in the beginning phase of a relationship. Yes, it's a hassle. It can leave even the most self-confident man second-guessing himself about what to say and how to act around a newfound female interest. But it's one of the "gotta do's" in order to reap the benefits that a good woman can bring you.

The Cheap Man's Special

The Second Date

Okay, Becky passed the myriad of tests that I put her through on the first date. Then I played a couple of head games, and talked to her on the phone a couple of times to let her know that I wanted to keep seeing her. Now we were ready for date number two. This is a relatively minor one in the grand scheme of things. It is merely a prelude to the big potential that looms for date number three. Playing a lesser, yet still important role, the second date should always occur on a weeknight. Instead of doing something extravagant, this date should be spent at home. Maybe just hang out and rent a movie or catch some tube. But make the meeting at her house rather than yours, if possible. This way you can take the lazy man's way out and not have to bother cleaning your place. More importantly, she will feel more comfortable at her house because it doesn't have the same sexual implications. This allows you to save your place for the third date when you will be more likely to make your sexual play. Also, if you are at her house and things start to go awry, you're only a convenient excuse away from being out of there.

This date is important because you get to find out how the two of you get along during a normal evening at home—we'll call this one the Mr. and Mrs. Cleaver Test. This situation, in which you, sitting home alone, would be bored to tears and questioning if you indeed have any semblance of a life, is a good proving ground for any budding relationship. If she makes an ordinary night enjoyable and it seems that she could even make an insurance seminar a good time, then she definitely will make new strides down the long-term relationship path.

This average-night-at-home type of evening is also a good indication of how your married life together might be. It is a well-known fact among single men that once you get married, you and your spouse immediately become two amorphous blobs of goo joined together at the hip without a creative or exciting thought between you. Maybe, just maybe, if she is so much fun that you even have a rockin' time sitting around doing nothing, your married life together will be more rewarding than the 4th grade piano lessons that your parents forced you to sit through.

There are also some key points to experience on this second date. This is where your level of comfort with her should allow you to do things like giving her a little tickle when she makes fun of something that you say or do. As your hands cause her to laugh and squirm, does she: 1) Totally shut you down and say, "Stop that or the elbow near your groin will have you singing a soprano version of "Moon River" before you can whistle the first note of Dixie?" (That's definitely a bad thing.) 2) Does she go along with the tickling and tolerate it for a while before saying, "Let's just watch the movie?" This is better, but don't write home just yet. 3) Does this one tickle turn into an out-and-out battle that takes you through four rooms, a pillow fight, non-stop laughter, and possible loss of bladder control? Lock her up, throw a white dress on her, and look for anyone that even remotely resembles a Justice of the Peace—now!

Spontaneity, under ordinary circumstances, is the key. I want a girl who isn't afraid to act like a complete moron just to make me laugh. I would like to have someone who I could slave over a fine candlelight dinner for, only to end up going out to eat after we have a food fight with said cuisine that could rival anything that a lunch room full of sixth graders could do. I want a woman who can get the sleazy diner patrons in a town similar to where Deliverance was filmed to believe that we are genetic researchers investigating reports that people who eat sausage links produce offspring that have no nostrils. This is someone who stares society's stringent norms in the face and says, "Back off, pal. There's a serious rebel inside this woman." Of course I would like her to be able to do all of these things yet also fit in at the stuffiest of stuffed-shirt gatherings and appear to be enjoying herself. Easier said than done, huh?

I haven't seen Becky in action at any corporate shindigs, but she's definitely got a solid grasp of spontaneity. After seeing a commercial that mentioned the Declaration of Independence she started singing the Saturday morning cartoon song that put the pre-amble to music. I joined in and before we knew what hit us we were dancing around her apartment to our personally generated tune. Combined with the numerous times that I got in some hearty belly laughs during the evening, I'd say that having fun with her on any stay-at-home evening would be no problem. I also felt very comfortable being with her. Sometimes when you're not doing something that provides a constant source of conversation, things can start to drag and you find yourself saying something that is about as earth shattering as the noticeable lack of dust-bunnies under the couch. With Becky it was just the opposite. Because of our unending conversations we probably didn't catch more than a few lines from the TV shows that we watched. In a world filled with mundane people it is always good to find someone interesting to talk to. Unlike some women that I've dated she doesn't shove words out of her mouth just so that her ears have something to listen to. She told me a lot of personal things and I enjoyed listening and learning about her life. I found that the more that I got to know about her, the more I enjoyed being with her. That was definitely a good sign.

There are a couple of other major points to consider before we put old date number two into the history books. The end of the date should consist of some tender moments of cuddling, kissing, and general slap-and-tickle kind of stuff. Feel out her physical boundaries as to what she thinks is appropriate. Does she maintain two zones on her body that will result in amputation of the culprit limb when they are touched? Maybe just one zone? Maybe she only turns your hand away when you attempt to move inside the clothing? Women are all different on what is too much or too little, but at any rate, don't try and do the nasty on the second date. Hold out until the third date to make the swing for the big home run. She'll be impressed that you had her alone and didn't make the big play on her, and that will give you some nice-guy brownie points that will definitely be valuable down the road when you inevitably piss her off.

Close the evening with a nice gentle kiss, a smile, and some comment stating how much you enjoy being with her. This is a good time to throw this in without the fear of her thinking that you are moving too fast. This set-up all leads perfectly into the all important third date. Finally end number two by detailing the candlelight dinner and romantic evening that you have planned for Friday night's scheduled third date.

I played it up a bit with Becky so that she had the rest of the week to create the fantasy in her mind and build up her expectations. When I gave her the play-by-play on how Friday night would progress she seemed to be really looking forward to the date. I didn't mention my sexual expectations for the evening; however, I would have to just play it by ear with that. From date two's discoveries it appears that it was possible. Though I made sure not to let things get too hot and heavy, she never put the brakes on me when I started letting my fingers do the walking. I'd just have to wait and see on Friday. I started to look forward to it quite a bit myself, but so far, I couldn't wait until the next time I saw her. I just hoped that it would stay that way as things moved forward.

To Be Carnal, or Not to Be Carnal

Sex Enters the Relationship

You can go one of two routes for big date number three. If you are capable of creating something better than hamburgers or macaroni-and-cheese on your own,
cook the meal for her at your house. If cooking isn't your forte, take her to a nice,
quiet place that has the proper ambiance (that's French for "a restaurant with table
cloths"). Either way you should cover a few necessities in preparation for the
evening: 1) Buy her roses. Whether you get a single long stemmed rose or a dozen
depends on your cash flow and/or the degree to which you want to impress her; use
your own discretion. 2) Go a couple of steps above the level of your normal attire.
You want everything about the evening to symbolize its significance. 3) Do all of the
chivalrous things that women want you to do—open doors, pull out chairs, and do all
of the other little niceties that will make her feel special. Everyone likes to feel pam-
pered now and then, so why not go all out? However, draw the line at taking off your
suit coat and laying it over a puddle. That's a made-for-TV act of chivalry that is not
required by even the most discriminate female. Your local dry cleaner will be just as
happy as she will be when you walk her around said puddle.

Hopefully all of the special things you do for her will pay off later in the night.
Make sure to have wine or her preferred alcoholic beverage with the meal. Alcohol
is a great aphrodisiac. The addition of an intoxicant to a date will always be positive

51

unless she's a card carrying AA member. After a couple of glasses of the vino' have entered her system, float a couple romantic and sexual comments by her and gauge the response. Also a few sincere compliments or a comment about how nice her eyes look in the candlelight won't hurt.

Now comes decision time. The unspoken rule of dating among the hip, happening, nineties crowd is that the third date is the sex date! You've built up some feelings for each other during the first two dates, so now it's time to bump things up to a new plateau. Before you make your play, however, you should analyze whether getting horizontal is a possibility. Think back to how she responded to your physical advances when you had her alone on the second date. If she's said previously that she likes you, but there is no shot in hell that she will get naked and interlocked with you until you're married, chances are you shouldn't go ahead with the plans for sex tonight. At the other extreme some girls have dropped the old standard of "waiting until the planets align" to do the wild thing, and you might have already consummated the relationship on dates one or two. Use any signal that she's given you up to this point to help figure out if sex on this night is possible. If you are in doubt, go for it. She'll shut you down if things get too hot and heavy for her, but women expect men to be oozing bags of hormones. Most likely she won't hold it against you, and you can apologize by saying something like, "I really care for you and I just thought it would be OK to share our feelings for each other by making love, but if you are not comfortable with that yet that's all right." By saying this you will keep her from harboring any lingering resentment about your sexual play. That is important to prevent anything that could derail the relationship.

Many people do indeed go for the bump and grind on the third night. That is why you need to make sure that everything about the evening is perfect. A lot of romance, some obligatory comments to show how much you care for each other, and a quiet relaxed atmosphere are important—you want this night to be as memorable and pleasurable as possible. You want it to be a night that will still bring a smile to your face (and hers) when you are old and gray. It should be a night that reminds you of the commercials for diamond necklaces during the Sunday night movie that try to hawk you a $20,000 number that you really can't afford.

After dinner go back to your place for another glass of wine and some more quiet conversation to keep the evening flowing. (To make myself look even more thoughtful I remembered her favorite wine from the wine tasting tour and had a chilled bottle waiting in the refrigerator.) For those people who are not fortunate enough to have wineries nearby, if you subtly ask what her favorite wine is and have a bottle on hand, that will be sufficient. Then slowly ease into the physical end of the spectrum. Take it slow; this isn't "Beat the Clock" night. Assuming that the date started around 7:00 p.m., it will only be about 9:00 p.m. at this point. This means that you have about five hours before the desire to sleep overtakes your desire to fornicate one more time—be patient.

There is one universal law that you must obey during this part of the evening to ensure your chances of sexual success. After making out for a while you must give her a back rub. (Asking her if she would like a back rub at this point is like asking a drunk if he wants a shot of whiskey.) This will also give you an easy way to get her shirt off if you explain that it will feel much better if you touch her bare skin with your hands. Having a bottle of baby or massaging oil on hand will also help make the rub more sensual. This is a relaxing, yet stimulating part of foreplay that will help to ready her body for the upcoming events. This is also a good activity because even the most ungraceful male is capable of making a back rub feel pleasurable. The only thing that you have to do is to find out what level of firmness she prefers, and rub until she's totally relaxed. Remember that leaving permanent imprints of your hand in her skin is a good indication that you are pressing a bit too hard.

Her responsiveness to the back rub also is a good indicator to how far you'll be able to go with her. If she puts on her parka before you start you can bet the farm that you're in for a cold front. But if she offers to take off her shirt count on a warming trend. After this the rest of the night will just flow naturally (body fluids included). Provided that you take it slow and find out what makes her feel good it will be a stellar occasion for both of you.

Just remember, after you do the big deed the relationship has changed forever. To women this first act is more important than mall grand openings, dieting, and good hair days combined. So be ready for some big changes afterwards. Falling asleep immediately after the culmination of the act is not recommended unless you find pleasure in receiving swift jabs to the kidneys. This is a time when she wants nothing else in the world more than to cuddle and talk about all the sacred things that women hold back until after they are intimate with a man. Expect her to be more affectionate than a stray that you bring in from the rain. Go with and enjoy it. Hell, that's what tonight is all about!

The only thing to watch out for here is to make sure to walk the tightrope between saying things that imply too much or too little commitment. Even though she feels like the dam that held back all of her love emotions has just burst, don't get too comfortable because what you say can and will be used against you in the court of love. And remember, all's fair there and in a fox hole. Also be sure to agree with whatever she says if you want to wake up alive. If she tells you the sky is purple, tonight it is. Tomorrow's a different story, but tonight, the phrase "me too" should grace your lips as frequently as possible.

If she asks you questions that require you to actually take a stand on something, when in doubt, be vague. This way it makes it harder for her to cite your comments in the future with specific references, and it makes it much easier for you to say, "You must have misunderstood me. What I really meant was…" By taking the middle ground on anything that you talk about, you are free to scale up or scale down what you actually meant by 50% in the future if/and/when it is needed. This is very important given the new ground that has been broken tonight. The relationship is now at the point where you can sit down, put your feet up, and say, "I'd definitely take this over Sunday football, any day. Well, except for the Super Bowl, but that goes without saying."

Sex is definitely a wonderful thing, and it is much more meaningful when done with someone that you care about than with someone whose name you barely remember in the morning. Caring about your bed partner also makes you more giving during the physical build-up to the main event. The slam, bam, snooze routine gets replaced by a good deal of touching, caressing, and a need for her to hold you like a baby.

With Becky it was better than any sexual experience that I have ever had. After the culmination of our first sex act we just laid together in an embrace for what seemed like hours. I had feelings of being totally at peace with myself, her, and the universe in general. This is much different from my usual desire to say good-bye and sleep that I normally have after a sexual experience is completed. I also noticed that during sex I thought more of how to please her than I did about how to get her to do the things that provide me with a sensory smorgasbord. I now have a feeling of emotional closeness to her that was intensified during and since our first "insert Plug A into Outlet B" electrifying experience. As much as the sex changed her feelings for me, it altered my views about her as well. Whoever came up with sex definitely stumbled onto a great concept. Let me tell you, if I were Adam, Eve would have been too busy getting out of her fig leaf to have even thought about eating any apples.

When Ms. Right Meets the Idiot Crew

Introducing Her to Your Friends

At this point, things with Becky were generally copasetic. I knew that I was com-fortable with her and that she liked me. So just like in 9th grade math class when $3X = 9$ became too easy, it was time to introduce a new variable into the picture—could she tolerate my friends? In my case, it was important to wait until after we "consummated" the relationship to introduce her to them because being intimate with her lowered the probability that meeting them would cause her to say "these people are just too screwed up for me to put up with—it's over" from around 70% to some-where in the upper 20s.

She was so enamored with me after our third date that she naturally wanted to do something with me the following night. This set up the perfect opportunity for her to meet the idiot bunch while still maintaining my control in the relationship. I told her, "I've already made plans to go out with my friends, but you can come along if you want." This statement says to her "Yes, I want to spend time with you, but I'm not dropping everything and moving in with you because of last night."

In my mind I was actually saying "Everything is perfect so far, and I really like this one." I just had to hope that none of my friends would do anything like ask if her mother puts out, or comment to her about the things they would like to do with her, an open mind, and a bottle of Wesson. Most of all I prayed that they didn't get drunk and decide to have a contest to see who could come up with the slimiest and lowest thing that I'd done in my life. But I couldn't hide her from them forever. It was time to get it over with.

The date which will always be remembered as "The Night Ms. Right Met the Morons" went as follows. Being the eternal gentleman, I picked her up at her house and brought her back to my place—the gang's meeting spot before heading out on the town. I was impressed by the fact that everyone was on his best behavior, but the night was still young. They'd have plenty of time to nail me to the cross later. One beer down, as we waited for everyone to come over. Some idle chatter was passed around. Two friends asked her why she's going out with me, and one friend pole-vaulted across the line of good taste with a crude remark about women. Before I met Becky, I would have been the one making that comment, but on that night I was cautious, just hoping that they didn't offend her too much. When everyone arrived, we took the usual 15 minutes for introductions and discussion of where to go, only to decide to spend the evening at the same local bar that we always graced with our presence. Everyone except me volunteered not to drive, and we filed out.

At this point I wished that a couple of my married friends were with us. It was only going to be a matter of time before the guys started their normal party-time behavior. Having a few other couples around would have put a tighter leash on the single guys. This would have also given Becky and me someone to talk to when they inevitably started hunting for anything female that walked upright.

We hung out with the boys, drank a couple beers and, of all amazing concepts, she didn't have an overwhelming urge to slap all of my friends for their rude comments. Somehow she liked them and thought that they were funny. Now I knew that this girl was incredible (or at least just a bit weird). They took to her as well, and I even got a congratulatory "thumbs up" from one when Becky had her back turned. Soon their beverage-induced desires started flowing. Out came a couple of comments about how much they'd like to see certain girls naked and hovering above them, and my wonderful date suddenly realized that she had an unusual opportunity to see how the other sex lived. Tonight she would get to view bar life through the eyes of men on the prowl. She endured and even enjoyed it. On that Saturday evening she was involved in something totally different from her normal night and she still found their words and actions humorous. In contrast, I displayed a much calmer, mellower version of my normal self. I was busy preparing for her inevitable question "Do you act just like they do when you're out?" When that frightening query finally came, my reply had a joking tone as I said "No, I always acted just like I am now. That's how I met a great girl like you." She knew that I was full of it and that I would have been the ring leader of the horny bunch if she wasn't present. But my present actions were what concerned her, not my past. Besides, even though she thought that their unending quest for beer and babes was a bit peculiar, she was still enjoying herself. She understood that they are men. Hell, we're supposed to be horny every waking minute.

Being with her helped me to discover some of the advantages of having a date with you at a bar. First, there's no such thing as rejection when a slow dance comes on. Fifteen minutes to closing time doesn't produce the feelings of urgency and despair as the prospect of going home alone becomes evident. And most of all, I got a general feeling of happiness from the fact that I was having a great time with both my friends and a woman that I cared for. It also gave me a big old grin as I saw my friends getting rejected and then planning ways to talk to any available woman in the bar, knowing that I didn't have to play that game.

The night passed and despite the friends' actions and one's imitation of a dog with his head out the car window on the way home, she liked me even more. After emptying the reject bus, she and I headed back to her house to close out the evening. She was a bit playful on the way home, and the night ended in the sexual arena just like the previous evening. Another hurdle was crossed on this date, and things were still moving in the right direction.

Becky and I had those first four dates under our respective belts, and we were still going strong. This little thing was gathering steam, and I'd have to bet that soon the boyfriend/girlfriend phrases would be flying more frequently than United Airlines. We'd just keep letting things progress and see if it would lead us to love, or if a month down the road I'd be back to the bars looking for a new woman to take down the dating path.

Easy Boy, You're Getting Serious

Going Beyond the Run of the Mill Relationship

"We're going out!"
"Those two are dating."
"Pete's only riding one pony?"
"Yes, we are seeing each other."
"Believe it dude, I'm going monogamous!"
"What does she see in him anyway?"

These are just a few of the colorful phrases that you start saying and hearing as you venture forth into the wonderful world of coupledom. It's that big bridge you cross when you begin to realize that you've found a person with whom you can spend some quality time—one who is getting straight A's on the myriad of relationship tests and one whose company you enjoy even more than the average grandmother likes knitting sweaters.

This change in the seriousness of my relationship first hit home when someone I knew saw me with Becky and asked that question guaranteed to make any "newly-dating" guy shudder in fear. "Is this your girlfriend?" Jason and his hockey mask could never make a chill go up my spine that fast. The sweat poured off my palms like Niagara Falls, and my heart was beating louder than a Metallica concert.

My initial thought was, would she think I was getting serious too quickly if I responded with a definitive yes? Did I take the easy way out and say that, "This is my friend Becky?" Hell no! She would have not only been offended by the fact that we had five great dates (two of which included carnal knowledge) and I said that she's not my girlfriend, she probably would have gone on some psycho-crazed tirade and tried to beat the crap out of me. Well, I had to go for it and say a big yes. I even threw in a gentle squeeze of her hand and a smile for added emphasis. This response went over much better than flatulence in church. She replied with a smile and a reciprocating hand squeeze. One small step for mankind, one giant step up the commitment ladder.

The assumption here was that if she was looking for wedding bells somewhere down the line, I had to forge ahead in the commitment department. While I wasn't trying to blaze the trail into "I Love You's" after five dates, I wanted her to know that things were progressing and that my feelings for her were getting stronger each time I saw her. This kept her feeling confident that things were going well, and if she was happy with our relationship she'd go out of her way to keep things moving in the right direction.

I had been noticing that she was flashing some commitment signs too. They were simple things like her saying, "I was telling my girlfriend about what you did the other night and she thought it was so funny" or when she introduced me to a friend and I got the statement "So you're Peter!" It's always good to know that the girl you've started to spend time with doesn't want to keep you hidden under a boulder somewhere.

Another good boost for the male psyche is when a woman takes the lead role in planning a date. The first time that she calls you, plans the whole evening, and asks you to be over at a certain time—that's a big positive in my book. Not only does it make the average man happy that she's overcome the barriers of assertiveness to plan an evening, but it shows self-confidence in both the relationship and in herself. Besides, just like being on the bottom during sex or waking up Sunday morning to find the festering mess from last night's party all cleaned up—it's good to let someone else do the work sometimes.

But now that I was at the "Yes, we're dating" stage of the relationship, life had it's share of differences. Gone were the endless string of weekday nights spent munching on whatever I found in the refrigerator that wasn't green and moldy. Gone was waking up on the couch to the sound of the National Anthem. Gone was going out for a few beers with the boys on a Tuesday just to see what type of person actually goes out on a Tuesday. And gone were the Sundays spent under a comforter on the couch, leaving that comfortable haven only four times the whole day. Two emptyings of the bladder and the intake of some non-nutritional crap food were all that was needed on the average Sunday. All a single man needs is a remote control and a cordless phone. Laziness is a wonderful thing.

Instead, when we watched TV, we rented a romantic comedy which allowed us to get in a few aaahhhs and a couple of kisses when it inevitably "all worked out in the end." That Tuesday night out wouldn't be to a dive bar, but rather to a play or something cultural, and Sunday—I'd be showered, shaved, and wearing more than the previous day's underwear under that comforter.

But, that was why I spent the endless Friday nights looking for this woman. Even though life was different it was worth the changes. Of course, while I was looking for Ms. Right, my friends that had already found theirs caught constant abuse including, "He's whipped," "Boy, he doesn't party like he used to," and "If I ever get like that over a girl, shoot me." This is all part of the single male psyche. When you don't have a girl, you say things like "I love the freedom of being single" or "I want to be able to come and go as I please" to make yourself feel content with your lack of a girlfriend. Remember the male credo: it's not how happy you are that's important, it's how happy you make people think you are. Really the whole time, single men are desperately searching for the great things that women do for their lives.

Now that I was well beyond those thoughts I had to face those same friends that two weeks ago I was arm-in-arm with bashing our "coupled" friends.

So what did I do when confronted with the same comments that I had been making about someone else a short time ago? Did I tell them about the trips to plays and the fun night we had laying on a blanket staring at the stars? Did I tell them about how good she makes me feel when we're together or the romantic evenings at home? Did I dare comment that I'd found a great woman who I enjoyed being with even more than I liked hanging out with them? Nah, I did the only thing that a self-respecting man could do and replied, "Well, at least I'm getting it regularly from a good looking girl. What about you?" That shut them up for a while.

It seemed that the more that Becky and I experienced the couples' scene, the more I found myself shying away from those detractors who were jealous of my new-found happiness. This was partly because I didn't want to face the continual hounding about finally becoming monogamous, but mainly there was only so much time in a day and now she had the top billing. I did, however, decide right from the start that I wouldn't spend every waking hour with her. I needed to save some time for myself to do those things that kept me on an even keel. That helped me to sort out how I felt about her as things grew. If things did work out I'd have plenty of time to spend every minute with her after the wedding bells, so I made sure to keep a night out each week with the friends. That way I don't miss out on who was sleeping with whom, who vomited on a family housepet and what wild escapades happened last weekend. Also, as much as my friends may piss me off at times, girls come and go, but a good friend is forever, and I didn't want to lose that. Although the girl will have priority in the long run, I wanted to maintain all of my friendships because they'd always be very important to me.

Speaking of friends, I had also noticed that after about a half dozen or so dates with Becky, my married or coupled friends went from being people I only called if I was really bored or needed to borrow money to friends closer than me and little Jimmy were when we spent everyday in the sand box at age 7. Now, these people who were boring because their ideal Friday night wasn't hanging out at a hoppin' bar searching for fresh female flesh were a great time for the "new" me. They were even "preferred" company because the women could talk to each other and discuss the skirt style of the year and I wasn't bored to tears because I had someone to talk college hoops with. Also if I wanted to shoot some pool or do some man stuff, I didn't have to worry about Becky being bored just standing there watching me, because she'd be knee-deep in a conversation with my friend's wife or date. The situation lent itself to keeping everyone happy.

Another good thing about going out with other couples is that you don't feel that you have to continually tame your touchy-feely instincts around them as you do when you're with single friends. While single guys are against affectionate displays unless your date is willing to commit those same acts with them, friends in the other category not only accept these acts, but they subconsciously encourage them. This atmosphere also lends itself to a lot of sexual talk between the couples. Even though women tend to be squeamish about discussing sex in public, get a few drinks into two women who get along well, and they will say things that would make a gynecologist blush. This is another one of those puzzling tidbits about women that we men are not meant to understand.

I had gotten myself "up to the butt" in this serious dating mind set, and I'd made some necessary lifestyle changes in the process. Now came what every man looks forward to about as much as a rectal examination—meeting her parents. This is the epitome of "getting serious." Was I ready and actually willing to subject myself to a night of intense scrutiny from her Mom and Dad? What other time in your life provides you the opportunity to have someone you don't know pass judgment on every part of your life from your long-term career goals to your choice of socks for the evening? This is done with a level of sheer boredom that could only compare to a marathon Lawrence Welk festival surrounded by a room full of denture toting grandparents. And for what? Well, it was a good way to ensure that I'd keep getting it regularly! But, yes I spent this one night under the microscope to further the progress of this relationship that I'd started. My only hope was that her parents were like her and not the parental units from hell. My goal was to leave them with a good impression, and not give them cause to ostracize their daughter from the family and cut her pictures out of the photo albums because they felt the guy that she was dating was an unequivocal loser. Would I succeed? I think so.

The evening started with a feeling of looming discomfort. To them I was someone that could possibly ruin their daughter's life, cost them thousands for a one-day party at which some rings would be exchanged, then inherit their life's savings when they die. So, I guess they had every right to analyze my words, actions, movements, and table manners during the entire evening. In this house I was guilty until proven innocent. This made me nervous. In my efforts to impress the hell out of them I was prepared to reduce my personality to the level of sheer banality that I normally reserved for talks with a priest or people over ninety. Remember, no matter what the season, choose a sweater on these occasions—never let them see you sweat.

Though I appeared to be my usual calm self, my feelings of tension made me feel like I was in the dentist's chair. Taking on the attitudes and mannerisms that were last seen in "Leave It To Beaver" with the hopes of winning the approval of people who were generations away from me and who would immediately send their daughter to the monastery after only five minutes of stories about the real me was definite cause for a tension headache. Even my normally cool date showed signs of strain as she started up seven consecutive conversations with the phrase, "Mom, do you know that Peter...". Each of the previous six died a bloody death when the four of us simultaneously ran out of things to say and found it an opportune time to simultaneously eat another forkful of dinner.

Despite numerous occasions during the evening when you could cut the tension with a machete, all in all, it was a success. From the moment we caught them peering out the front window to see if I pulled up in a 1978 Duster only to smile when I didn't, until my closing statements on how the Mrs. could come cook at my house anytime she wanted to, I made a good impression.

The secret to meeting the woman's parents is this: everybody is nervous, but act like you're not bothered by it. Make some safe jokes. Make yourself look as good in their eyes as possible. Take a few opportunities to dish out compliments and positive statements about their home and the world in general. Whenever necessary embellish a little to make yourself look even better. Do all of these things and they'll immediately want you as a son-in-law.

For example, current job: "I sell cars."—Wrong. "I'm in the executive training program with a large automobile manufacturing company."—Right. How did you two meet: "She was at a local bar looking kind of desperate, and I was pretty horny. So I took her home, put the wood to her and the rest is history."—Big Wrong. "This may sound a bit corny, but the night that we met I saw her beautiful smile from across the room and I started staring at her. I watched her for a minute and noticed a certain friendly air about her, and when I started talking to her later, I immediately realized that she was just as nice as I had imagined. Things have been going great ever since."—A bit wordy and very fake sounding to you and me, but trust me, they'll eat it up.

It's like a job interview, facing your father after you crashed the family car, or any of life's other very unpleasant moments—tell them what they want to hear and you'll be in business. At the same time, don't make yourself out to be the King of Spain. Be honest about yourself and what you believe in—just throw a coat of whitewash on your ideas and normal language. This will put you in a better light without the need to fabricate events or life stories. You just have to be very careful of the things that you say and do. But if you think about it, to a lesser extent, you do that in the beginning stages of a relationship anyway, so this dinner thing is a piece of cake after a handful of dates with the same woman.

When I did get to the point where I didn't worry about what I said and did in front of Becky and went back to my normal uninhibited male self, that's when the warning flag popped up and slapped me in the face. I had passed into the serious relationship zone. I noticed that I didn't always do those little "open every door for her" type of things anymore. I was at least two dates past asking her permission to change the temperature control in my car, and worrying about swearing in her presence—that had died a grizzly death long ago. Not to say that I became a belching caveman whenever I was near her, but there are certain niceties that you add to your personality during the first few dates that quickly diminish as soon as you become comfortable with a relationship.

As I got closer to my normal persona when I was around her, I started to think—how quickly should I start letting her know about my bad qualities? Over what period of time should I spread it out? Do I throw in another one about every week or so, or should I push out a group of them each time I know she's really happy with me. Maybe I should make a "bad qualities" agenda: tonight she sees lazy, I bite my nails, and I'm a bit overconfident of my abilities. Next week I'll give her a dose of I eat food that is bad for me, I'm financially irresponsible, and I leave wet towels on my bed in the morning. By the end of the month if she still likes me, then I'll know that she can handle anything. Likewise, I'm sure that I'll soon get to witness some of her less desirable qualities up close and personal, as she starts to let them descend onto me like a pallet of bricks.

It is at this point that all semblance of reason and rationale starts to disappear, and it is your feelings that are the guide for determining if you could spend a lifetime with her. You find that her traits, attractiveness or six figure earning potential are not important anymore. Your feelings are what turn into love, and they are the glue that holds things together through life's trials and tribulations.

Of course Becky's similarities to the ideal woman that I dutifully laid out for you a few chapters ago did help to move up the "getting serious" ladder a bit quicker. If she did lack a few qualities, however, I could have easily chosen to ignore them, given that all powerful "halo effect." I had found that despite my efforts to find her faults in my tests early on I had gotten to the point at which I would go out of my way to see her good qualities rather than focus on the bad. When I couldn't find reasons that I shouldn't keep dating her I started to realize all of her good qualities. I might have even been guilty of putting her on a pedestal, but it's better to strive to see the good in someone rather than the bad.

Did you notice the about-face in my attitude here? Before I found Becky and started getting close to her, you saw the untamed wild attitudes and urges of a single male. Throw a good woman into the equation and even the most he-man-woman-hater calms himself down. Of course, as a member of said group, I would fight, claw, bite, bend, fold, spindle, and mutilate to keep from admitting this to my friends or anyone within earshot, but rip off that facade and I knew that it was true. It hit home one Friday night when she was tired and fell asleep in my arms. After I looked at the clock and saw 11:10 p.m., I had a serious mental awakening.

Not only was I sober and laying in bed before midnight, but I was soon to be asleep at least five hours before the **Guide to Hard-Core Manly Partying** suggests. Worse yet—I didn't even try to salvage my pride and at least stay up a few hours having sex. What was in store for me? Would I find out what was on the other networks during Monday Night Football because she thinks it's too violent? Would I drive 10 miles in a blinding snowstorm at night because she decided she wanted onion dip? Would I do everything from breakfast in bed to wiping her nose because she felt a sniffle coming on?

That did it, as much as I had to use my hands to guide my mouth to say it, "I was wh-, I was whi-, all right I admit it—I WAS WHIPPED!" I hadn't seen my friends in three weeks, I didn't walk around the house in my underwear, I didn't even burp aloud just because I liked the way it sounds. I was beyond hope. I was gone. My voice went up an octave when I talked to her on the phone. I enjoyed spending time with this girl more than I had ever enjoyed being with a person, I had a great time in my discovery of all those "couples" things to do on the weekend, and I was happier than I ever had been.

This is where the thought of becoming the type of guy that men make fun of temporarily consumed my brain and caused the "relationship relapse." During this short time the grass suddenly seemed much greener on the other side, and a three round bout with self doubt, disbelief, and desire for dusk 'til dawn delirium just like the old days overtook the thoughts about how great the relationship was. At that point of mental anguish I asserted to her that "I'm going out with my friends, and I want to go without you because the guys can't do the same things when women are around. Besides, if you went I would spend all of my time with you and I want to hang out with them for one night since I haven't seen them in so long." I also remembered to smooth things over by stating that this had nothing to do with not wanting her around so I can pick-up other women. Forget this disclaimer and all trust would be shot to hell. I might have still gotten a 3:30 a.m. "I miss you…" call that night to see if I was home in bed where she wanted me, but I'd probably do the same thing and I trust her. It's understandable given the circumstances.

She gave me the green light to go our separate ways on a weekend night, and there I was out with the boys just like the old days. Bacchanalian bonding over a bunch of cold beers. Yes, this was the way life should be. It was simple: life straight out of a beer commercial. I quickly remembered the proper technique for sizing up a girl from head to toe without being blatantly obvious—it was just like riding a bike. Being back with the guys was like driving a Yugo. It ain't pretty, doesn't have any extras or frills, but it's cheap and simple. On that night my language, attitudes, and cares in the world all plummeted to the ground like the Goodyear blimp with a 10-foot hole in it, but guys' night out shouldn't be any other way.

The next phase of the evening started the manly ritual of scouting the people of female persuasion. We got right to the point of it—we were dogs in heat and we were damn proud of it. Something had changed though. This was when I realized my feelings for Becky. It began when I saw a woman who looked a lot like the one who was patiently waiting for me at her house, the one who I left for the evening to begin the foray into male bonding. I saw the look-a-like girl and a cascade of memories about my girlfriend washed through my mind. I was a has-been beyond his prime and out of his element in the sport of Championship Naked-Horizontal-One-Night Wrestling, but I really didn't care. Did Becky take my professional sleazeball status away?

The remainder of the night was not spent in a constant full-body examination of every available female as a prelude to a chance game of doctor. Instead, I did the weird things that I noticed my "coupled" friends do when they came out with us. I spent the night talking and laughing with whomever was refueling for their next strafing run at the available women. I was talking to my friends about life, about feelings, and of course we threw in some sports talk every now-and-then as a reassurance that we were still real live males. These conversations were the things that made us good friends in the first place, and it felt good to catch up on some old times. Along the way I found myself thinking and even talking about the woman who brought about this change in me. I had a good time, albeit a different type of good time from what I was accustomed to with the boys, but nonetheless a good time.

Upon being dropped off at home still under the influence of the evening's libations, it was I that made the phone call to her. A call to tell her I was home—home, without some big breasted concubine to conquer for the evening. A call just to hear the voice that I missed tonight. Of course, I can't say that to her. The control factor was still lodged in my brain. When I called, I couldn't be all sappy and tell her that going out with the boys wasn't like it used to be. The key here was to reassure her while still maintaining my feeling of self-control.

First, you have to sound drunk. Drunk just implies that you had more fun than a great white shark at the U.S. Underwater Swimming Festival. Second, tell her how much fun you had. It says, "Yes I am trustworthy and come home alone, but I can still have a great time out with the guys, and should I ever desire to do it again in the future you should have no objections. Next you can come out with the "I missed you tonight. Let's do something fun just the two of us tomorrow night." These two statements give her peace of mind. She can now feel at ease that your feelings haven't changed and that you still want the relationship to keep moving forward.

When I did call I really just wanted to talk to her after a night apart. I admit that I was a bit whipped, but there's nothing wrong with that. I had what I was looking for all along and it had made my life happier. I could only hope that things would continue to progress the way that they had started. She was definitely a keeper. She had more potential than a stacked beauty pageant contestant who sleeps with all of the judges. We would keep climbing that commitment ladder and see where the relationship would take us. I was taking it one day at a time with both eyes open wide and looking forward. And though I hoped that the foundation that we'd laid for the future would be constructed into a strong and beautiful building, I wasn't letting my judgement be obscured by the great emotions that were overflowing in my mind. If the relationship started to change for the worse or fail, I would be wise to it. But at that point it showed no signs of problems, and I had great expectations of what the future would bring.

Even More Serious?

Enter the Deep Emotions

Time. It stops for no one, flies when you are having fun, heals all wounds, and does more cliché things than the Brandy Bunch combined. Time is what it takes to keep jumping through those relationship hoops like a circus poodle during the Saturday night show. A certain period of time must pass before the pet names start flying through the air, before she loses the name she was given at birth only to be referred to solely as "my girlfriend." And yes, even though your favorite sports team is playing in the most important game of the season, it is not as important as helping her move furniture.

Time is the guide that determines the course and the place of the commitment path—or at least that's what Becky said. She wasn't ready to go away with me for the weekend without making up a cultural event that we'd be attending to appease her questioning parents, but we were a good two weeks past using the bathroom separately on a Saturday morning.

Personally, I think her "time scale" idea is whacked out enough to be part of David Koresh's former cult, but why start an argument over something as simple as that. Emotions and the way that you feel about each other should be the factor for determining what point you are at in the relationship. If we both feel like we've hit it off well enough to make the all important jump to monogamy after only three dates, then damn it, we should do it. Putting time limitations on something like this is like penciling "have sex" into the 11:00 p.m. to 12:00 p.m. time slot in your daily planner. Contrary to what my friends might say about it, 11:00 p.m. to 11:05 p.m. would not be sufficient time for me to complete this activity. All-in-all, this scheduling of emotions to determine what is too fast or too slow is a point that we disagreed on.

Becky and I established great communication channels that allowed us to gauge our feelings about the relationship at any given time. By doing so, we minimized the friction that occurs if both of us weren't on the same plateau on that "mountain climb to love." Though this communication helped to make sure that we were on the same page, our relationship developed so naturally that we just seemed to stumble into most things without even thinking about them. Spontaneity. It's the key that helped to make our relationship fresh and full of life. That's the way it should be. Yet she still held back on certain things because "It's just too soon to be doing that."

I'll give you a prime example. She was involved in another relationship that ended just prior to our humble beginnings. This made her timid about making too many statements of affection. Those schmaltzy "I enjoy being with you," "I have such a great time with you," "I love your smile," are heard only if I do something really special, or if she was under the influence of some carbonated alcoholic beverage. A couple of drinks make her more affectionate than a three-week-old puppy, so needless to say, Friday night has usually been our most enjoyable evening together. In contrast, I can never hear these things too much.

Her reasoning for not being overly sentimental is that she feels that constant statements of affection will lead to emotions disguising real feelings for each other on a friendship level. She thinks that this will screw things up in the long-run, so she continued to hold back until some unknown time despite the fact that she had the same intensity of emotions that I did.

There is some validity to her logic. I get swept up in the emotions sometimes, especially after things happen that bring us closer. Still, it seems too mechanical playing by her rules. It's almost like "Man Meets Woman," brought to you by IBM. I don't agree with her, but I do see her point and I haven't made a big deal out of it. So there, I did it—I still have my own opinions, I disagree with her instead of blindly caving in to her simply to eliminate friction. I'm not just a hollow shell of a man living for her beck and call.

The relationship should be 50/50. Men sometimes have a tendency to let themselves be dominated to keep the woman happy. As you get closer and her demands of you increase, you want to show her how much you care as a means of ensuring that the relationship will keep progressing. Even as she makes these requests for us to wait on her hand and foot, this isn't what she really wants. A spineless jellyfish isn't the person that she first became interested in. Someone who lives solely to satisfy another person's every need is boring. So we should not be afraid to tell her "no" when she wants us to drive 50 miles for goat's cheese because it is lower in fat than regular cheese. She will just have to make do with the cow variety.

This will sometimes lead to that inevitable "gray area" about what type of request is outlandish and what things a thoughtful caring boyfriend should do. This is normal in any relationship. An important tip for rejecting her request without making yourself look like an insensitive oaf is to never say anything along the lines of "I don't feel like it." That says to her that you don't care for her enough to even attempt to satisfy her wishes. But saying "The time that it will take me to get the goat's cheese will take away from the time that we have together. Spending time together is more important than a couple of grams of fat." How can she argue with that reasoning?

This shows that you care about getting the most out of the relationship instead of thinking strictly about yourself. And you should think this way. If this girl has potential to be your other half someday, then you should start looking at things in terms of satisfying both of your needs instead of focusing on your individual desires.

When this type of scenario has unfolded with Becky and me I've noticed that my initial thought was to justify my actions by showing her the benefits that they provided us, and she appreciated this. What I felt was not a rationalization for my own self-interests, but instead was a genuine desire to feel a mutual happiness. I noticed that this happened more often the further down the relationship path that we went. We both have individual needs that we would like to have satisfied, but we respect and care for each other enough to think of the other's needs. Sure there are times when we don't get what we want, but I always know that her rationale for not catering to my desires is not a selfish ploy. Instead it is her judgment that our energies could be better spent in some other arena that would provide our relationship with more benefits. When we have differences about the importance of our individual desires we talk through them and determine a solution that takes both people's needs into account without personal hidden agendas. That is another of those many things that I enjoy about our connection.

Rather than bottling up our negative emotions, we subscribe to the policy that it is better to communicate differences no matter how trivial they may seem. This is another example of the give-and-take process in action. It is also part of the reason that we don't have knock-down-drag-out fights. Instead, when we have differences of opinion or when one of us does something that upsets the other we remain calm and discuss these problems rationally without the need for kicking, biting, and screaming.

It allows us to constructively accomplish our objectives, and it prevents us from saying those things that we can't take back that usually come out in a fit of rage.

I recommend this philosophy for anyone to use, not just with your partner, but in all relationships. If you can exhibit the self-control to not let your anger get the best of you the communication channels will be much more functional to solve the difference at hand. It also serves as a calming factor if someone begins a tirade against you. Their emotion will soon diminish when they notice that you are not taking a combative tone with them, and the discussion will mellow to a less emotionally charged level. If you don't currently react to emotional outbursts in this way, try it with someone—you'll be glad you did.

As my relationship with Becky progressed we discovered the concept of "ebbing and flowing" (no this has nothing to do with monthly female cycles). It relates to how the emotional attachment between two people increases as time passes in a relationship. Once you get past the first month or two of the bonding ordeal, you start to notice that days or even weeks can pass when your feelings for her seem to grow faster than a kid does during puberty. Other times they hold constant or even dissipate slightly. Obviously every minute that you spend together isn't going to be the most fun time in the history of the world, and you have to expect problems to come about. But, you also have to continue to evaluate the causes of the negative ebbing, so that you can learn how to avoid them in the future.

When you get close to someone and begin to sense her moods and feelings, you can also get a good approximation of what is bringing about their ebb or flow. Many times the bond that you have with them will bring about a corresponding ebb or flow in you because of the effects that their behavior has on the intensity of your feelings. If she's spewing venom from every pore when you see her, chances are that your feelings for her won't go spiraling upward at the speed of light. Likewise, if she's very affectionate, fun to be with, and you feel like a kid at Disneyland when you are with her, emotions may start climbing that hill towards love at a pretty good clip.

The key at this point in the relationship is to attempt to find ways to maximize your partner's flow while minimizing the ebb. What does she want you to do when she's in a bad mood? Does she want you to leave her alone? Does she snap out of it when you start joking around with her? Does talking out her problems help make her feel better? It's all a trial-and-error process and you have to find out the best way to handle her various emotional states.

The other type of ebb that can be encountered at this point is the old female standard of "I need some space." This occurs if she feels that the seriousness of the relationship is more than she can handle at the moment and she would like some time to sort out her emotions and where this thing is heading. Usually it is best to let her have the time alone and not be pushy or try to coerce her into working through the problem with you. If the relationship is as strong as you think it is, she'll be back to normal soon. Having had a chance to analyze her emotions she'll gain a new appreciation for the relationship. The important thing is to let her know that you are willing to give her the time and space that she needs and that you will be there to talk whenever she needs you to.

On the other side of the coin, when she is flowing—go with it. Use these opportunities to do some of the wilder or more unusual things that you didn't think she would go for a while back. If she is the one for you, she should be the person that you have more fun with than anyone. So when you are clicking together do special things that will make this time together even more enjoyable than usual. Hopefully, as both of you gain more experience in dealing with each other's patterns, you will be able to better survive the strains of the relationship and you will gain an additional appreciation for each other when things are going good.

When learning about her pluses, problems, and pratfalls you will inevitably come across some small ones that are weird, mildly messed-up, or at least, incredibly bizarre. When she knows that the hooks are entrenched deep enough into you that you won't haul your butt right out of the relationship, that is when she shares her idiosyncrasies with you.

Becky is no exception. I don't know what or why, but she derives a pleasure from squeezing the acne on my back. Allow me to set the record straight; I'm not a breeding ground for oozing pustules, but like most men, my back has it's share of minor acne outposts. If she catches me off-guard and bare-naked from the waist up she's got a hobby that could occupy her for hours if I don't put a stop to it. I now realize the power that a female has when clamming up and closing shop on a horny boyfriend. That type of feeling that you get from shutting down something that your partner enjoys is mine when I turn and shelter my back from her onslaught. She may say pretty please, but I still keep her mining efforts shut down. I have to draw the line somewhere.

For me this isn't a problem of relationship-ending importance. In fact, if she wants to spend time "pore-poppin'" it's no skin off my back. If it makes her happy, then it's no big deal to me. Everyone knows that I have enough quirks to fill Freud's notebooks. The peculiar things that she does don't bother me, though. We all have some unusual habits and behaviors—it's what makes us human. I guess being abnormal in these little ways is, for lack of a better word—normal. If she didn't do anything weird or didn't have the self-confidence to do things outside of society's so-called proper behavior, I would be more worried about her.

Time for some more introspection as I inched closer to actually being in love with this girl after only a few months into the dating world. Looking back at my life in the pre-Becky days, I noticed that I changed in many ways due to her influences on me. Granted, I still went out with my friends and I enjoyed whooping it up on the town despite the fact that I usually ended up thinking about her at some point in the evening. And I was still quite far from the point where I'd be willing to slip a ring on her finger and be joined at the hip forever. But I definitely saw great potential here. We were a good third of the way up the relationship ladder and the rungs were coming closer each time.

It was evident to me that I was beginning to see the effects that a woman can have on a man and how they manifest themselves in every-day living. I felt that I was moving into a different phase of life. I'd moved on from the wanton sex-fest of the last eight years and had come to a new point which was more enjoyable and much more sedate. I'd found that my body was balking at the little sleep/big hangover lifestyle more and more prior to meeting Becky. So this change was something ushered in by my body as much as by my mind. But, the relationship's calming effect on my mind made me feel better too. Having someone who is there for you certainly minimizes the lonely nights and keeps you from wondering if there isn't more to life than rear ends and weekends. She had given me added stability that kept my life more balanced. The picture of my future filled with responsibilities and a woman who depends on me looked very fuzzy a couple of months back, but after some adjustment to the contrast and V-Hold buttons, it was starting to get a bit clearer. I actually looked at this next step in life not with a fear of change, but with expectation for the challenges of something new. I wasn't there yet, but again, I certainly saw the relationship's potential.

Sex Talk—Straight from the Hip

Some Insights into Everyone's Favorite Topic

A llow me to hazard a guess as to what people hope to get from reading this chapter. The average testosterone-laden male is waiting to read about some lecherous sexual experiences to help him re-live his past exploits. A couple of radical feminist groups are looking for any excuse to picket me, the publisher, and anyone who looks remotely like me. And many of my past sexual partners and their lawyers are standing by looking for any incriminating statement that will allow them to suck every penny out of me. Everyone else just wants to see how many miles beyond the line of good taste I'll actually go. Well, ready or not, here it is:

Let's start with the most talked about sexual difference between males and females. Women want to delay having sex until they feel that their emotional bond with the male is strong enough, while men want to hold off about an hour (the same time frame as going for a swim after you eat). Why is this? From what I've seen, there are a couple of reasons. On the guy side, let's first state as a fact the obvious—all orgasms feel incredibly good! Every male that I know well enough to discuss this type of thing with will freely admit to at least an orgasm a week since soon after puberty. Of course, with the exception of one friend (and the jury's still out on whether he's desperately lying out of a lower bodily orifice), we are not all fortunate enough to have had a woman to share in all of these sexual experiences. So we take matters into our own hands, and despite certain rumors—no one that I know has gone blind as of yet.

It's a physiological thing. Men need to have orgasms with about the same frequency that babies need new diapers. One friend of mine who adamantly denies ever being a member of the "Sex for One Club" provides scientific proof to the physiological need theory. He stated that he would have a wet dream once a week or so if he was not getting it regularly. A one-person study: Is that an accurate scientific theorem or what? Even if you don't buy into the physical need idea, which I will go to my grave defending, everyone will agree that people do need some means of sexual release regularly. Given the fact that the two-person version of sex feels much better, we males go out looking to commit the sex act with members of the female persuasion as much as possible. Granted, sex is more intense and rewarding when you are with someone who you have strong feelings for, and the threat of venereal diseases should temper our urges somewhat, but most men would rather have sex with a less-than-perfect partner for the night than go home to an empty bed. This serves to fuel the fire of promiscuity that runs rampant in the male population.

This urge for sex that we have a great difficulty controlling has also caused many men to do some things that they thoroughly regret in the morning. But as I said before, this urge does have a physiological basis—it's not just our male egos in need of stroking as women would like you to believe. In fact, for all of you men reading this book, let's pause briefly. Set down the book and think of the most ridiculous thing that you've done in your life for no other reason than you wanted to get laid. I'm serious—sit back and scan your memory from the early teen years until now. You will probably come up with at least five occasions that make you chuckle or hold your head in shame.

The reason that we act so stupid when it comes to sex does not end there. The other cause for male sexual behavior is that multisyllabic word called—socialization. We are taught from day one that men are stronger, we are the bread winners, we must take the lead in relationships with women, and that promiscuity is a part of being a man. You see it plastered all over the media, the arts, and even the bathroom walls. How many times have the ladies seen "Call 232-5123 and ask for John. He puts out for anyone" in a girls stall. The reverse statement about Jane is on most every men's room wall from Maine to Hawaii. This socialized attitude about sex has many harmful side-effects, and mostly it serves to propagate the sexual behaviors of the average male.

Now for the female side of the coin. Before I begin, I will attach a disclaimer by saying that I am not a female nor have I ever been one, so I cannot speak about their internal feelings and beliefs. Instead I speak based upon the actions and conversations with many females with whom I have discussed this subject.

Unlike males, most women do not orgasm every time during sex. Many women orgasm rarely, and some never. This is partly due to self-built mental dams that women put in their minds which block the flow of their sexual river. Many women need an emotional attachment to their partner in order to remove this barrier. When they are having sex with someone that they care about, the mindset involved with sex will release the river. Difficulty climaxing can also be attributed to the inability of or lack of desire by the male sexual partner to do the things necessary for her to attain orgasm. Therefore, a man with which a woman has a strong emotional bond will increase the probability that the mental part of the equation necessary for her to orgasm will be present. Also, if her partner cares deeply for her he'll be more likely to spend the time and effort doing the physical things needed to march her toward "the promised land." Hence part of the reason that women try to resist their own sexual urges is to hold out until a time more likely to increase their enjoyment of doing the "naked and horizontal."

Also, the socialization that teaches men to be promiscuous is reversed for women. Just as the male is praised for sleeping in more beds than George Washington, the female who does the same gets the "scarlet letter." This is something that looms in the mind of a woman when the normal sexual urges and a persuasive male come into the picture.

So put these sexual differences together and what do you get? Sexual friction, the need for prostitution, some of the reasons why people aren't compatible in the sack, and more Geraldo episodes on sex than you could ever want. In addition, you get yet another reason why maintaining a long-term male-female relationship can be more difficult than discussing early Greek philosophy with the average canine.

The key to making the sexual part of these long-term relationships more successful is simple. It, like many other facets of the relationship, requires that both people constantly communicate their needs and desires with each other. I know a couple that talks freely about every other aspect of their relationship, yet when it comes to sex they discuss their problems with the frequency of the coming of Haley's Comet. Why? It is because the sexual taboos regarding open discussion of sex with our partners that our culture has dictated keeps them from doing so.

In today's society we make numerous references to sex and talk about it freely with friends, but when it comes to openly discussing it with our partners, our mouths are clamped tighter than a guy's butt cheeks on his first day in prison. If it truly floats your boat, why not tell your partner that having sex in public bathrooms is a big turn-on for you? Why not share the fact that doggie-style sex is more pleasurable to you because it allows deeper penetration? Tell her some of your sexual fantasies and then act them out together. Chances are she'll enjoy the change of pace and it will help keep the sexual part of your relationship fresh and exciting. If it happens that your fantasy is too crazy for her realm of acceptability she'll nix the idea, but what have you lost in process? Nothing. If everyone was able to communicate their sexual desires as well as they talk about what they want for dinner many of society's sexual tensions and dysfunctional behaviors would be reduced.

Think about how difficult it would be to say "Mom, do you prefer missionary position or do you like to climb on top when you and Dad go on your weekly sex romp?" Most people are disgusted or horrified at the mere thought of this. But why, I ask? You would have no qualms asking your parents where they met or what attracted them to each other, so why is there such a big hang-up about them or anyone else doing the deed? The fact that we are alive automatically requires that they have indeed gotten horizontal together (adopted children aside). I guess that the sexual revolution hasn't hit our parents' generation. As adults in the '90s, we should not be bogged down by old taboos. So whatever it takes—discuss all aspects of sex with your partner.

We also shouldn't be afraid to discuss our sex lives with our friends. I have learned a great deal about sexual activities and creative new ideas by discussing my endeavors with my close friends. These discussions are not the Sunday-morning-boast-fests with the boys in which exaggeration is the name of the game. They are serious one-to-one talks with friends that I can speak with honestly about my sexual practices and pit-falls. All that it takes is to put aside the macho mentality that no one is capable of teaching you anything about sex, and to not be afraid to admit your sexual shortcomings. I myself used to be such a quick shooter that I could have easily beaten John Wayne in a sexual gunfight. I think my sex gun was so amazed that it was actually being used, that it went off before the female had a chance to change her mind about doing the nasty.

After some initial apprehension about discussing the problem and the bruising of my ego that it took to get the words out, my friend gave me the advice that cured me of it. In this case it was an extreme emotional build-up in my mind that got me so excited about doing the bedroom boogaloo that by the time the act actually came about, I was ready to shoot without hesitation. Of course my partners were not too pleased with this, but during my one-night sex days, pleasing the partner was not necessarily a sexual requirement. I found that if I relaxed and did not place such a premium on having sex, that my premature emancipation of the sperm was conquered. By not being as excited about sex, I actually made the sex better. Strange, but true.

This simple, yet important discovery was made possible by getting past the taboo of discussing the problems and complexities involved with sex. It's funny that as much as everyone thinks about, talks about, and has sex, we don't take more time to learn how to do it better.

Especially the talking part. We talk about sex a hell of a lot more than we actually do it. It could be a locker room discussion of last night's sexcapades, a bar room talk of how much better the tight-skirted babe across the bar would look on you than the clothes that you're wearing, or even a simple smile when a friend prods you about your level of sexual activity with a newfound female interest. Whatever the situation, all red-blooded men on our planet love discussing sex.

Note to any females who haven't written me off as a sexist pig by now and are still reading. If you have a one-night experience with a guy, prepare yourself for the fact that all of his friends will soon know everything from the unusual things you did during the lustmaking process, to any tattoos or birthmarks you may have, and the sexual attractiveness of the parts of your body covered by a bikini. But before you women say "That's disgusting; sex is not something to talk about.. It's private." Just admit it—females chat about it with their friends too. You might not get as descriptive or embellish the stories as much as we do, but you talk about it with the girls just the same. It's natural. If you can't "sex and tell," then what good is doing it. Well, OK, there are still many good reasons to do it, but sharing the gory details certainly makes Sunday mornings more fun.

There is one point where most guys, including myself, draw the line. It is not right to divulge your sexual history about someone that you are currently involved with. The minute that it's over, that's a whole new ball game. Then you can't wait to share all the explicit details with your friends—especially if she dumped you. This gives you the peace of mind that if she's going to rip your heart out, at least everyone will know about all the sleazy things that she did in the sack.

When a girlfriend is involved in the discussion, even the most heralded warrior in the "Capture, Conquest, and Conversation" game bows out of the stories about the power of his mighty sword and the creatures it has slain. It feels wrong to share intimate details about someone that you have deep-seeded emotions for. I didn't think that my Sunday morning talk-show "The Babes in My Bed—This Week in Review" would ever go off-the-air, but it has and I'm proud of it.

It's another one of those personal changes that I have made because of my relationship with Becky. I feel great when I think about how good our sex is, but I think

I would be betraying her if I shared our sex stories with my friends. I also believe that I would be grouping her with all the one-night women I've had if I gave details to the boys. Lumping her in with that sordid clan is something that I definitely don't want to do. The way that I feel about her is so different from the faceless, nameless group. I think that everything I do with her, the way I feel, and the way that I act around her should be totally different than the women that came before. Turning over a new leaf am I? I guess I've learned a useful tidbit of information about myself. When it comes to serious male/female relationships the respect and feelings that you have for your partner are revealed in many different ways.

The role that sex plays in my relationship with Becky is much different from my past as well. It's far beyond the "I'm bored; let's screw."

"Why?"

"Because it's fun."

It is still a very pleasurable experience, and I very much enjoy the way that it makes me feel, but now it has an added dimension because of the emotional bond I have with her. When the act first begins I feel an emotional intertwining much greater than the obvious physical link. With one-night sex my body had some great physical responses, but as soon as it was over the feelings were extinguished quicker than the fire-department could put out a barbecue grill. Now the emotion is actually greater after the culmination of the act. There I lie, physically spent, still wrapped in the arms of someone I care deeply for, thinking how good she makes me feel. To then express these feelings to her and hear her reciprocation gives me an inner-peace that is beyond comparison. Though I don't regret the countless physical encounters that I had before this "spiritual" one, I see now why sex that has strong emotions attached to it is much more rewarding. That is the real joy of sex.

I hope that it will always remain this way, but I realize that the more time you're with someone, many different problems can throw a monkey wrench into the well-oiled sex machine. I'm readying myself for any potential difficulties before they occur. No matter how minor they may be, we make sure to openly communicate with each other any problems we are having in the sexual arena. So far this has worked like taking Vitamin C every morning. You don't know how many ailments it prevents, but you keep taking it because you haven't gotten sick yet.

Of these sexual problems that could occur in the future, a few common ones immediately come to mind. You'll find that the causes and solutions are so easy to figure out if you are able to see them in their proper perspective.

1 The girl doesn't orgasm during sex. Time to communicate with each other on how to get her mind into the game. Most likely either the guy isn't doing the phys-

ical things that are necessary for her to have "the Big O," or she has a mental block that prevents her from doing so. As much as men hate to admit it, it is usually just that we males don't do what it takes to make her scream. The easiest way to avoid this is to catch the problem the first couple of times that you have sex with her. Tell her in advance that you are going to find out how to make her feel as good as she can, then spend an entire night finding out what she likes and dislikes throughout the various phases of sexual play time. Don't let the male ego interfere and take the attitude that you can make every girl go nuts during sex and if she doesn't then it must be her problem.

Every woman is different. Things that make one woman scream like a banshee, another could hate. Ask her what makes her feel good. Unless she just came down from the hills to avoid being a virgin sacrifice, chances are she'll have a good idea of what is pleasurable to her. Use her reactions to your various touches and caresses to sense her level of enjoyment in the build-up stage. If you are gentle in the beginning stages of foreplay, then progress slowly through each sexual area. This will help her to ease into the emotion of the event and allow her mind to help her body build up to the big finish. Unlike males, who can be ready for sex with one sex-charged statement out of her mouth or a glimpse at her tan lines, she needs more time to get ready.

Once you spend some time gently touching and some clothes are shed, you get into the real foreplay. Allow me to get technical and graphic to show a very important point. Just like doing your homework helped you get good grades in school, you have to do your prep work to be a straight-A sex student. Here, the advance work consists of going the oral sex route. Most every woman has a much easier time orgasming during sex if the man does some mouth work before hand. I know that for some guys this is against their code or is something that is desired as much as a pick-ax in the skull, but this is one of those give and take situations. Learn how to do it just the way she likes, and she'll be eating straight from your palm forever. Couple this with a finger gently moving up and down her sex device and she'll have the moisture level of the average rainforest well before you are ready to climb aboard.

When that important time does come, there are some other things that can help get her close to howling like a wolf. Numerous books have been written on this subject, but I'll attempt to give you my abridged version on how to put a woman over the edge. The most important thing is to find out exactly how she likes it. Does she want to be ridden like Secretariat, or cradled like a baby? Preferred positions, roughness, and pace all vary from woman to woman. I know a girl who would let you do whatever you wanted prior to sex, but when crunch time rolled around, she would flip over onto all fours because pooch-style was the only way she could orgasm.

Aside from these differences, there are a couple of universal things that help get women to the climactic point. First, once you actually start the sex itself, tease her, toy with her for a while. After you make penetration, she's more than ready, willing, and hopefully able, so take some time to help her build her emotions. Act like a unionized coal miner, and go in the hole for a while, come back out and rest, in for a minute, out and rest even more. This will serve to build her sexual frenzy while saving yourself for the constant motion to follow. Because we all know, that once a man starts that constant thrusting, he's only got a limited time before the sexual volcano erupts. This teasing helps to get a woman's mind anticipating and craving sex. Since the mental blockages and too short of a sexual duration are two of the most frequent reasons for her lack of orgasm, this teasing helps to build her mental expectation, while increasing the duration.

If this still doesn't get the job done, try rubbing pelvis to pelvis for a while in the middle of the event. Women are capable of orgasming strictly by rubbing or putting friction on the skin just above the vagina, so grinding hips without your penis going in and out much will help build her orgasm potential and also delay yours. If even this fails, try using your hand on her immediately after your groin becomes a useless sexual tool. Keep it going as long as you can in a further attempt to put her over the edge. If after all this, she still doesn't get there, keep experimenting with different things during foreplay and sex. If at first you don't succeed, you'll both enjoy try, trying again.

2 Another of those sex problems that can rear it's ugly head is the boredom factor. A lot of times when the male gets bored with his partner it is because he feels it is like riding a bicycle built for two and he's doing all the pedaling. Since men usually take the aggressive role in sex, some women are content to play dead and let the man do all the work. This makes the sexual excitement level crash through the floor real quick. This boredom can also occur if she's a sex hog—someone who wants you to pleasure her but who isn't ready to return the favor. This is another of those "talk it over" moments in the relationship that I've mentioned quite frequently.

Both of these situations show that either she doesn't have knowledge of how to be an active and equal-opportunity arouser, or more likely she doesn't have the desire to do so. People have a natural tendency to enjoy receiving more than they give, so if she is that way, you have to explain to her that she has to be more of a sexual Santa Claus. If it takes changes in your sexual routines to do so, you will find it more rewarding and chances are that she will enjoy the sex sessions more when you are satisfied anyway.

3 One partner wants sex more frequently than the other. Big generalization coming here—99% of the time it is the male who doesn't know the word "moderation" and wants sex more than the woman. I have known a few cases in which the reverse was true, but most of the time, it is the man who gets stuck in sexual overdrive. Reasons? There are many. First of all, socialization gets its hand in to stir up the cauldron of sexual desire. As I mentioned before, men are taught to take the dominant role in the sexual performances, and we are conditioned to want sex as much as possible.

So what do you do when she doesn't want it with the same regularity as you? No, don't break out the porno's as soon as she leaves the house—talk to her. Uncover why she doesn't want to do the bedtime bop as much as you. Chances are she might not enjoy it that much because A) she doesn't orgasm much during sex or B) as time wears on, sex loses it's appeal for her. We've discussed that orgasm problem already, but with choice B, you need to delve further into her psyche. Is she bored with sex in general, or just bored with romping with you? If sex in general has lost it's flair, the single beds that your parents sleep in can still be avoided by finding the physical things that she does enjoy and putting more emphasis upon them in your physical rituals. This may get her aroused to the point that sex will interest her more. If she just isn't into sex, and after discussing it, she remains steadfast in her resolve, then unfortunately it may be something you'll have to live with. If this resolve is something you aren't comfortable with, you must inform her of this. If you can't make a compromise that satisfies both of you, check into seeing a sex therapist so that you can come to a mutually agreeable solution. Sex is an important part of the relationship, and you both must be comfortable with it so that your problems in the bedroom don't extend into other parts of the house.

If it is strictly sex with you that turns her stomach, then either there's a much deeper problem with the relationship that you have to work through, or you need to change your sex technique to increase her satisfaction. If your preferred mode of sex consists of the "slam-bam-snooze" routine, you might want to vary or at least liven up the sexual agenda. If she's got an adventurous side or is open-minded towards new things, try oils, whipped cream, different positions, risqué locations, more foreplay, living out fantasies—take your pick. Find out what would add excitement for her and run with it.

There are many other complications and hazards that you can run into when it comes to sex. Those listed are just a few of the more common ones. By no means is this list complete. But one thing those problems all have in common is that they can all be solved by communicating openly and honestly with your partner. The sexual component of the relationship should provide fulfillment both physically and emotionally. A good sex life helps solidify your relationship's emotional bond by providing a tangible method for you to realize the feelings that you have for your partner. It's a great way to express how much you feel for someone by sharing a gratifying physical and emotional act with them. That is why this is such an important component in a successful relationship.

It is not the most important component, however, and your feelings for someone should not be dependent upon how good they are in bed. Relationships based solely on sexual compatibility quickly burn out when the rigors of every day life with an incompatible person strip away the pleasures that the sexual part of the relationship provides.

Sex also shouldn't be thought of as a relationship "Band-Aid." After the moaning and groaning of sex is over, the problems that you had before will still be there, and they will re-occur soon after the sexual euphoria wears off. The idea that sex solves any fights is flawed. Though it may replace negative emotions with positive ones in the short-term, it does nothing to deal with the causes of the fight and it doesn't teach you how to prevent the problem from re-occurring. Dealing with and solving the problems when they happen is the only way to maintain a successful relationship and to learn from your experiences. If you want to roll around with each other after taking care of the problem, then by all means slap bellies until your heart's content, but not until then.

Basically that's all I have to say about the act that makes the world go around. I hope you weren't disappointed by the lack of sweaty details about any past exploits and conquests, but that part of sex doesn't occupy my mind like it used to. The days when how good a time you had on Friday night was based upon how many sex stories you could tell Saturday morning have gone by the wayside in favor of a more tame lifestyle. Because of Becky, I've learned about the other side of sex. It is one that doesn't boast, need constant partner variety, and doesn't necessitate regular trips to the clinic. I've learned how much better sex feels when it is with someone you care about, and the advantage of monogamy that I never realized before. Chalk up one more plus for the steady relationship.

Saying "The Words"

Love Changes Everything

Picture this scenario—soon after accepting a new job your boss asks you to attend the annual company costume party. To earn some important brown-nose points that could be used to break a two-way tie for a future promotion between you and an equally qualified co-worker, you spend hours designing an elaborate costume in preparation for the journey into corporate partyland. With your expectations set on high you venture forth to the party aiming to make a good impression on everyone from the janitor to the CEO. Just as you are about to enter, out walks a man in formal attire who says a polite "Hello" as he passes. Your jaw collides with your knee in a fit of disbelief.

Is this some twisted corporate initiation to subject all new-hires to the humiliation of being dressed in a costume at a formal gathering? Will your ego be left on the party room floor swimming in a puddle of embarrassment? Quickly you regain your composure and assure yourself that the man was just the caterer and that you didn't miss the memo about the change of dress code for the occasion. Nonetheless, your heart races as you enter, and you are prepared for both the ultimate humiliation or an earth-moving sigh of relief when you walk through the door.

The same type of feelings run through your mind when you ready yourself for the climb to new heights on the relationship mountain. This is the plateau at which the phrase "I Love You" catapults you to a level that could give a nosebleed to anyone with even a slight fear of heights. It's like passing an 18-wheeler around a blind curve: Will you return unscathed to the comfort of the right-hand lane, or will you crash and burn in a fiery wreck? Only her response to your all important statement can determine which it will be.

I mentally prepared myself for the big event of saying "The Words" to Becky. We had just spent a fantastic evening together, and though I had been wanting to say the three words that would forever change the relationship for about a week, I had been holding off on my foray into "I Love You" until such a moment. I felt naked, bent over a table at the proctologist's office as I watched him lube up the rubber glove. I was defenseless, anxiety-stricken, and completely vulnerable. But I rounded up more courage than Oz's scarecrow could have ever imagined and said the words with an accompanying cautious gaze deep into her hazel eyes. My heartbeat—2000, blood pressure—20,000 feet below sea level, pupils—as big as grapefruits. All the vital signs were vastly different from my normally cool and collected demeanor.

But why should I worry? A lack of reciprocation on her part isn't the end of the world. It simply means that her emotions have not yet reached the same level as mine, but it won't alter our relationship at all, right? Unequivocal bullshit! It would be like California after a 9.0 earthquake—forever changed with no hope of exact reconstruction. If she starts giving me the explanation of how she cares deeply for me, but can't truly say that she loves me yet, then I know that I'm in serious trouble. I'll be doomed to a temporary emotional purgatory from which I can only be freed by her expression of her love for me. It will create a situation that is about as comfortable as a man donning burlap boxer shorts. I'll be second-guessing myself, analyzing every word that she's said to me in the last two weeks looking for anything that could have given me an indication that her response would be negative. Worst of all, I'll feel timid about saying anything further regarding my feelings until that point in time when she can honestly say that she loves me too. Disappointment that we didn't progress to that emotional level at the same time will set in, and she'll be left wondering why she doesn't share these feelings while simultaneously thinking that I'm trying to push the relationship too quickly. But, other than that, it won't make a bit of difference.

No, it is not the end of the world, but saying the phrase in itself is difficult enough. Having to add 15 minutes of downplaying and qualifying to the statement in an attempt to partially clothe your naked butt and reduce the fears and concerns introduced by the difference in emotional intensity—now that takes things right down to the level which can best be described by the phrase "That sucks."

So what did Becky do when I told her of my deepest heartfelt emotions, you ask? Did she softly repeat the words in an expression of her equally intense feelings, or did she leave me to rot, tied to a post in a rat-infested hell-hole? Much to my dismay it was the latter. My aspirations for the evening were left in a proverbial pile at the bottom of the emotional outhouse. Though she did her best to console me with how much she cares for me and how easily she could see herself falling in love with me, for the following seven days I had feelings of disappointment that came to mind whenever I pondered the event. I became more cautious about my choice of phrasing whenever I talked about my emotions, and I tried to avoid making statements that involved using the "L" word. She too was overly careful in that regard.

It is silly that one phrase has such stigma attached to it. We ride an emotional roller-coaster based on how much we hear it, and one well-placed "I Love You" can make even the worst day feel like an April day in Hawaii. Why is this? What makes one three-word phrase play such a vital role in our contentment? Why do we need the verbal reassurance when actions supposedly speak so much louder than words?

If you step back and think about it for a minute, you realize that it's simple. Love is the most powerful emotion that we know, and people are willing to do things for love that they would not even consider doing for any other reason. It is especially intense with your mate. Your love for this person is usually the most intense feeling in your life, and this love brings about more changes in you than anything else. So is this aura that surrounds that three word phrase justified? Absolutely.

No matter how much some people may adamantly tell you otherwise, everyone wants to be in love. The happiness and the confidence that it brings you are unparalleled. In fact, looking back at my sleazy days that seem like eons ago despite the fact that the calendar said it had only been four months, I remember that not having someone to love was the one thing that I was longing for. The lifestyle I had certainly provided me with a great deal of pleasure, but there was an emptiness and a longing that tore at me from inside. I wanted simply to be in love and to have the benefits in my life that love provides. I guess the great things that love does for you serves to explain why people do so many stupid things when love comes to town.

When your heart takes over it relegates your head to the passenger's seat and drives like a maniac out of control. This reckless driver can take you through the bad parts of town, down roads of jealousy, anger, and disappointment. But we let him drive anyway hoping that instead he'll cruise the picket fence neighborhoods of caring, joy, and compassion. The chance to feel these emotions with someone is what we strive for and why we are willing to put up with the negatives that sometimes come along for the ride. This love not only allows us to do many good things for the object of our affection, but it can inspire us to better ourselves by giving us the strength of a loved one to guide and reassure us when the going gets tough. Think about the things that people are willing to do in order to attain and cultivate the love of a relative or a friend. Now get out the algebra book and do some exponential work when considering the love of a mate. The degree to which we strive for romantic love is unequaled and helps to explain the origin of this stigma about "I Love You." The benefits love provides are different for every man and woman, but nonetheless, they are substantial. That is why everyone spends so much time looking for love.

That brings us back to my personal situation of love with Becky. Did she remain in a perpetual holding pattern, or did she ever land on the runway of love? It took her about another week after my "I Love You" folly, but she finally told me that she loved me and was able to pass the polygraph test in doing so. That made me both happy and relieved to know that we were finally on the same chapter in the book of love, and it strengthened the bond that we felt for each other. Now that I could finally begin expressing my feelings of love knowing that she felt the same way, it opened an emotional dam for both of us that flooded our relationship with some fast running feelings. Every now and then I caught her staring at me for no other reason than because she loved me. It's a good boost to the psyche to see and feel someone in love with you. For me, it triggered an emotional response in kind, and I'm sure that she caught me getting glassy-eyed at her a few times. After a period of emotional standstill and even some backtracking, we finally came to a point from which we moved forward again.

There's a lesson to be learned from this experience. When in doubt, wait! Wait to say "I Love You" until you know that she's right there beside you at this emotional checkpoint. Wait until there is no doubt in your mind that she'll tell you what you want to hear. Just wait.

I know that when this love thing takes over your mind that you want to tell her and every random passerby how you feel. However, this is another of those points of the relationship at which it will benefit you in the long-run to hold yourself back. It can end up doing more harm than good to the relationship if she's not ready to launch "The Love Boat," and this whole load of feelings of self-doubt and disappointment can be needlessly avoided if you do hold back.

If you really must know how she feels and would like to do so in a manner that doesn't require you to slice your guts open and sling them on the table there are a couple of sly ways of doing it. If you have the ability to read her feelings based upon her responses to the things that you say (and by now you certainly should) you can fish around for her view on love with a few well-placed casts into the pond. If skillfully done you can do so without actually committing yourself to saying "The Words." One good way to do this is to make a statement or two telling her that you assume that she loves you and then gauge her response. Any positive or negative feedback can help settle your mind on whether you can utter "I Love You" and get her reciprocation. If she clams up and doesn't give you any discernible reaction to go on you may have to resort to a more devious tactic—get her drunk and repeat the above procedure. Everyone knows that with a few cocktails in her gullet she'll spill her guts like an old oil tanker crashing against a shallow reef. Just make sure that when you attempt this that you keep your higher brain functions from succumbing to the power of the same beverages that you are feeding her, or it could result in a bigger mess than a 2-year-old, a pile of mud, and a white room could ever make.

If all of this fails and you still have a burning desire to know if "I Love You" is appropriate, simply force the issue when the time is right. Wait until some semi-sentimental moment and jokingly say "You love me don't you?" Now the ball is in her court and she has to respond one way or another. She might try to counter with "Why do you ask?" You can still avoid answering and maintain control by saying "Because I think you love me." The cards are all on the table at that point, and you'll either get a thumbs-up or thumbs-down in a matter of seconds.

Of course if she ever tries to pull this scheme on you, go one of two routes: 1) tell her the straight "Yes" or "No" answer that's she's looking for, or 2) take it as a personal challenge to your manhood to avoid giving her a straight answer. Assuming that she says all of the lines that were stated in the "force the issue" scenario, after she says "Because, I think you love me" this will bring about the ultimate male challenge. How do you get out of it without committing yourself, but also not piss her off in the process. When in doubt regain control with any rebuttal you can stretch for. How about "Well, I think that your only reason for bringing this up is because you love me." What a perfect come back to put the ball back in her court. If you were actually to compare this dialogue to that of two five-year-olds fighting over who gets the red truck and who gets the old blue one you would find some amazing similarities. But this is no time for rational conversation. Acting childish works here. Now that you've thrown her the curve-ball, she'll be forced to tell you her feelings first or drop the subject entirely. She'll know that the relationship isn't ready for the world of "I Love You," but she'll get this knowledge without having to make a verbal commitment. This allows you to both save face a bit.

Hopefully when the relationship gets to this point you can cross this bridge without all of this dodge and parry. However, when you and your partner are at this point in the relationship and one person does not have the same level of feelings, such gamesmanship can prove to be better than the let-down and set-backs that occur when one of you says "the words" and the other can't honestly respond in kind.

As for myself, even though I didn't get an immediate emotional ego stroking in the form of Becky's statement of her love, we did get to that point eventually. If I had it all to do over again I would have waited to say "I Love You" until all the ballots concerning her feelings were in and tabulated. Hell, I'm not perfect, I'll admit I made a mistake. I'm not quite to the point that I could screw-up a wet dream, but alas, to err is human and I definitely proved that I am mortal on this one.

That is another of those wonderful things about a love relationship. You can commit some high-grade faux pas and be forgiven without inflicting major harm upon the relationship. This quality that has trickled into our union, keeps imperfections or mistakes from diminishing our feelings for each other. The inevitability that you will not live up to the expectations of your partner in some situation makes it easier to deal with these mistakes when they occur. It also allows you to constructively communicate that the other person has made a mistake in such a way that allows both of you to learn from the experience and not to harbor harmful emotions. There is a pervasive feeling of understanding that is assumed as the relationship becomes more serious. It is one that hits home when you realize that this is the most important relationship in your life, so you had better do everything you can to accept minor mistakes and to honestly discuss the major problems. If this relationship is going to last a lifetime, let's lay the groundwork for an unselfish give-and-take interaction right away.

That is a part of the relationship that you notice when you fall in love. You know almost everything there is to know about the other person. You've experienced how they react in many different situations, and you have many good memories of the relationship logged in your mind. This allows you to accept some shortcomings, to know when she's going to react differently to something than you would, and to know what things she does that could bother you. But you understand all of these minor things and chalk them up to taking the good and tolerating the bad.

That's part of the reason why the volatility of the relationship diminishes at this point. You understand, accept, and prepare yourself for the mistakes that she may make, but you have the experience and the knowledge of what things that you do may bother her. This helps intensify your feelings of love because the smooth sailing in the relationship will make you even more comfortable with her and will serve to propagate these feelings.

A way that things can go awry at this point, however, is when one person takes a selfish outlook. If you assume that her knowing about and accepting your faults gives you free reign to do things that bother her, then you are setting yourself up for trouble. When you don't feel like making an effort to go out of your way for her you have succumbed to the "she loves me now, so she'll love me no matter what I do" mentality. This happens many times with couples who fight a lot. When one or both partners take the other for granted, and don't make efforts to improve themselves or to curb the behaviors that bother the other for the sake of the relationship, then things will start to go downhill. It's unfortunate, but it happens.

If you value the love that you have why not go out of your way to keep it flowing smoothly? Becky and I had our differences as any couple does, but when we did, we dealt with them constructively and learned from our mistakes. An example of how you can take your partner for granted occurred between Becky and me a while ago. I have a tendency to promise the world and not be able to produce it. I sometimes will make plans knowing that I might not be able to follow through on them, and this serves to get her hopes up, only to have them come crashing down when the plans get changed. After the third or fourth time that I did this she mentioned to me why this bothered her and that she disliked having to rearrange her plans around my ideas that don't end up coming to fruition. Instead of crying wolf, this boy cried, "We'll go out tonight. It will be fun." The solution was easy, I simply don't promise her things that I know I can't deliver on and eliminate the resulting problems while benefiting the relationship. Also I have since realized that I frequently do this with other people and I broke myself of this habit straight across the board. In essence, for the good of our relationship, I made a positive change in myself that has spilled over into other parts of my life. This example is pretty simple, but it demonstrates that striving to improve yourself for the love of your partner can allow you to reap many benefits.

I know what you're thinking. You've been reading the last couple of chapters, and you said to yourself, "Damn, Pete's reduced himself to a spineless, boot-licking, namby-pamby, jellyfish because of a woman. What happened to the real man that he used to be before this woman polluted his mind?" Yes, there is some validity to these charges. I admit it; I'm a changed man. Sure, I'm a different person than I was six months ago, but I'm a better person. I've adopted some of the ideas and attitudes of the woman I love. I've educated myself with a point of view different from my own and in the process improved myself. If you can't learn anything from or make changes for the person that you may spend your life with, there is something wrong with your relationship. I have gone through this transformation and personal growth because I am in love. No, I don't live to satisfy her every whim, but if I can make myself and our relationship better just by doing away with a few bad habits, then why not do so?

This person who you've become very close to also has the power to make suggestions that can lead you to self-improvement. By this point in the relationship she probably knows you better than anyone, so her suggestions aren't coming from left-field; they are coming from someone who loves you and who would like to see you become the best person that you can be. She has a vested interest in helping you to become this person. The more you improve yourself the happier you will become and voilá, in comes a person who will spread this happiness back to her.

This can only occur if the changes that she suggests are things that you view as improvements. Again, this requires that both of you are striving for the good of the relationship without overriding selfish motives. Hopefully you will not take offense to her suggestions, and will work to implement them knowing the positive results they will bring to your life. If you can do this you will find that the woman by your side can play a major role in your self-improvement picture. Of course if she's going to make these suggestions she will have to be able to receive them as well. If the relationship is everything it is cracked up to be that won't be a problem.

Maybe you never took the time to think about changes that occur in you and your relationship once you fall in love. As much as you may not want to admit it, when you're in love, you go through many of the same changes that I have experienced, and you receive many of the same benefits. Here's another one of those sit-back-and-think-to-yourself-for-a-minute situations. If you're currently in love think about the changes that you've made in your actions, your attitudes, and the relationship itself since you first said "the words." (If you're not in love now, think back to the last time you were, and if you've never been in love, then this whole discussion is pretty much moot right now, but re-read this when your Ms. Right comes along.) In thinking about this, you can probably identify at least five of these changes in your life.

You might have missed a couple of Sunday football games this year, you've learned how to have a good time on a Friday night without going out, and the guys' night out routine of drink-up, pick-up, and maybe even throw-up has lost its allure. Right about now there are some personal changes that you can also fess up to. Your attitude towards women is more accepting and understanding. You're more expressive and open about your feelings for her and of life in general. And you are finding that your trust in her is hitting a record high. These are good things. They help you to not only feel better about the relationship, but they also help it to grow stronger.

At this juncture the more obvious changes start whacking you on the head too. Those friends that used to be weekend mainstays now call you less and less because they just assume that you'll be out with the woman. By now you have established some set routines with her and have a few standard evening agendas that you can fall

back on when in need of a good time, and much to the dismay of the forever the bach-
elor part of you, every now and then you catch yourself thinking about a long-term
commitment and even (better sit down for this one) marriage potential with her.

After you cleanup the movement that the mere thought of matrimony just brought
about, think of how you feel when she says, "I Love You." When the phrase first
becomes part of your daily vocabulary it has the frequency of brushing your teeth,
maybe once in the morning and once before bed. Soon she starts sneaking in a couple of extra ones, and you find that your ego gets a boost of energy each time she says
it—sort of like that post-workout Gatorade feeling that you're supposed to get after
chugging it down. When you get to the point that you feel like a fitness instructor
detailing the daily workout "Give me 5 to 7 daily reps of 'I Love You,' 10 to 15 reps
of physical affection, and at least 20 kissing repetitions," then you know that you are
long gone. In the bag, signed, sealed, and express mailed.

So now that you've been forced to look at yourself in the mirror, cut me some
slack cause you're probably just as bad as I am. You just didn't realize it, or worse
yet, didn't want to admit it. There's nothing wrong with it. In fact it's normal. If this
change is made for love's sake and it benefits you, then it will benefit the relationship
also. Any two people can pound the Posturepedic, but it takes two people that really
care for each other to nurture a successful long-term relationship. These changes help
the existing bonds that you have for her to become stronger, and it makes those love
hurdles easier and easier to jump.

I've found in my travels that I am more in tune to Becky's feelings and moods
since we've made the jump to love. My gauge of her feelings is in full operation now.
It enables me to sense how to act around her, and it maximizes the time that we spend
on the same track. She does the same for me, and I find we almost always work
together to keep the flow going. By communicating our problems and concerns, while
expressing our happiness and positive feelings for each other, we keep the proverbial
ball rolling.

Continuing this down the road will keep the relationship moving in the right direction. I've learned not to be afraid of getting closer to her. If you love your partner and
you think that she is the right one for you, the relationship will progress a lot easier
when you constantly work at it. Couples that get lazy, think of their individual needs
over the needs of the other, or take their partner for granted make failure come easy.
Find what works for your relationship and keep working at making the bonds
stronger—that will help keep the boulder of love off the rocky road.

The most important thing to remember about love is that above and beneath all the
fluff and the fringe benefits it is a friendship. If you strip off the sex and remove the

physical affection you should find your best friend lying next to you. That is something that people often forget. The sex, the security of having someone who loves you, and having someone who enjoys doing things for you can sometimes hide some deficiencies at the root of the relationship. If you don't have a good friendship established, after the initial thrill of it all wears off, things will start to sputter and eventually fail. Take some time to think to yourself "Do I enjoy her company more than that of my close friends? Do we have serious conversations about our feelings or is Wheel of Fortune our deepest topic of discussion? Do I trust her when I'm not around or do I watch her like I would a drug addict in a pharmacy?" It is important to be able to answer "yes" to these questions since they deal with key components of friendship.

Although all of the qualities of friendship are important, let's spend some time on trust. You probably are finding that your trust for your partner has changed quite a bit since you fell in love. You don't ready your boxing gloves every time she talks to anyone who has testicles. Both your conscious and sub-conscious minds have begun to realize—this woman really digs me. I can trust her. Off comes your mental leash around her neck. A night out with the girls is no problem, her male friends don't pose a threat, and even a guy who starts conversation with her in a bar is no worry. She'll blow him off and come back to you. You're secure with her feelings for you and because of this you've put the jealous beast into hibernation with only an occasional stirring. This is another one of those building blocks for the future. If you are always looking over your shoulder wondering what she's looking at you won't be able to look forward.

If you instead choose to keep this jealousy routine going, she may shut herself off from every male on the planet just to appease you, but it will build a barrier in the relationship because she won't feel that you trust her. She'll probably still do the things that you don't like when you're not around anyway. But at any rate, if you trust her and have confidence in the relationship then why even bother with jealousy?

When you do tame your jealousy you will find it easier to give her more freedom to do the things she wants. One big perk here is that the more freedom you give her, the more you'll get in return, so for those who are still not convinced that being selfish is a bad quality, a big bonus comes attached to this one. It also benefits you when the additional freedom that you give her helps her to become more self-fulfilled. If she's satisfied with her life then you can bet that she'll be a lot happier. Optimally, you should give your partner this freedom but stand beside her to support and help her to reach her goals. Whatever these goals may be, if you are there to assist and guide her, both of you will benefit.

Time for one more journey into the workings of the mind of this former party-animal. I thought back to when I was hot in pursuit of Ms. Right, and I spelled out what I was looking for in a woman in a thorough, ranked order that would have made a drill sergeant proud. Upon pondering those now I realize that the things I wanted were what I was looking for before I really knew what I wanted. Translation: I fell in love, but I didn't do it because she had a bunch of qualities in precise allotments. I fell in love with a person, not her traits. Although Becky does have a lot of the qualities that I wanted at that time, it is her whole self and how she interacts with me that has changed my mind on love.

Love is amorphous. It's not like building a house. Its foundations are not of wood or concrete but of feelings and emotions. You can't lay down a blueprint of the person who you will fall in love with and what tasks need to be accomplished in order to do so. Certainly there are things that you can do along the way to help get the relationship to the point of love, and there are many more that will keep it progressing once you get there. But a genuine love is something that cannot be forced or coerced. It has to happen as a natural progression of feelings between two people over time. The house of love can be built however you would like, but it takes two people to build it.

I've acquired this knowledge the only way you can—I've lived it. Learning how to love cannot be done any other way. I can give my insights about it and warn you of the potential pratfalls you might encounter on your way there, but love is definitely a "hands-on" learning experience that no one can do for you. It's different for everyone, but one thing about it is constant—love will bring you difficult moments and give you times of self-doubt, but true love is definitely worth any negative that comes with it because its benefits are unparalleled in any other part of life.

Yes, I've changed. I've made changes in my personality, my attitudes, and my ideas, but most importantly I've changed my picture of love and what falling in love is all about. That is the most rewarding change of them all.

The Fine Art of Staying in Love

Avoiding Emotional Fallout

Nine out of ten adult love relationships last less than a year. The average person has five unsuccessful relationships before getting married. And over 50% of all marriages end in divorce. These statistics paint a pretty grim picture of your chances of having a successful relationship in contemporary American society. Why do relationships have such a high failure rate? Because people don't know how to deal with the problems that every day living brings and many times the partnership ends up crumbling under the stress.

Hell, any fool can fall in love, but it takes a special bond between two people to stay there. This is evident not only from the data above, but much more so from the many couples who obviously are not in love yet stay together for comfort and convenience. How many times have you heard older couples say that they stayed married only for the sake of the kids? With all of the different things that can put your love on the rocks, maintaining the ultimate emotion for a lifetime can be harder than getting an Amish person to wear electric-orange pants.

Whether it is too much fighting, a sexual problem, or simply that the relationship has lost its spark—things can go awry for many different reasons. Keeping love on the right path takes a combination of patience, consideration, and understanding. If you balance these things, add a lot of communication, and even throw in a bit of luck, a lifetime of happiness and its rewards can be yours. Some hard times and difficult challenges will stand between you and this happiness, but knowing how to identify and deal with the many different types of problems when they occur will allow you to better ride out the storm.

Of these many challenges to a harmonious relationship, keeping everyday life from getting boring is one of the most difficult. After a year or more into the relationship the euphoria of falling in love starts to wear off, and for the first time in the brief history of your partnership things can start to become routine. You don't always have something to say to each other anymore, and the vast list of things that you always wanted to do with a loved one has dwindled to things like touring the Spam factory or visiting kind old Aunt Mabel. So what can you do to keep your relationship from becoming about as exciting as a PBS documentary?

There is no universal secret for keeping things fresh and enjoyable. Certain things do help, though. As I've mentioned before, having a good friendship with your partner is very important. There may not be fireworks going off in your head every time you are with her, but the newness you once felt should be replaced by the comfort and happiness that you get from having your best friend by your side. Best friends talk about how things are going at work, tell each other about their goals, and share secrets they don't tell anyone else. They are glad to help when things go wrong and help you celebrate when things go right. If you find yourself reluctant to do this with your partner something in your relationship isn't right. If you have no interest in hearing about her day—something's wrong. If you don't want her to share her problems with you—something's definitely wrong. And if you find yourself going out to a local bar to watch tractor-pulls because that's more enjoyable than spending time with her—something's really screwed up. Successful relationships don't last a lifetime because she's a good cook or because she looks good in a bathing suit. They last because two friends enjoy each other's company, and they are willing to work at the friendship in order to foster a caring, loving bond that grows over time. If you don't have this in the relationship the boredom and other problems will come much easier.

If your friendship with her is sagging don't chuck in the towel just yet. It's not too late to firm things up a bit and to ease the boredom at the same time. Find some common interests to help bridge the gap. Way back when, I told you about a friend of mine whose wife took up tennis because he's addicted to the sport. Now they not only have a joint hobby that they both enjoy, but also one that gives them the opportunity to spend some quality time together during which they get a change of scenery, some exercise, and the chance to take out their aggressions on a fuzzy little ball instead of each other.

Every couple shares some common ground. If you take a few minutes to talk about the things that you enjoy, chances are that you'll find a few that are on both of your lists. If for some reason there aren't, try detailing things that you've always wanted to try, but never have. There must be some commonalties there somewhere. Sharing new or mutually enjoyable experiences is the foundation for building any friendship, and it certainly will help to bridge things with someone that you already love.

Being open-minded about trying new things is important here. Regardless of your geographical location and money supply there is always something new to do or try if you're willing to expand your horizons. Take weekend road trips, try activities outside your norms, and focus on appreciating the little things in life when you are together and life will be much more enjoyable. Hiking in the hills when the leaves are turning, canoeing on a peaceful creek, camping in the woods—they are all cheap, fun, and don't pose too much of a threat to the male machismo when done with your significant other. "Communing with nature" can really relax the mind after a stressful week at work and can bring the two of you closer at the same time. Hell, throw in some quality sex behind a tree in the middle of "Yogi Bear Land" and you will bring easing the boredom to a whole new level.

If you don't take these preventive measures to keep the relationship out of the "yawner files" other harmful situations can enter into the picture: two-timing, fooling around, gettin' some extra, and flesh dictation with the secretary. Whatever you want to call it, infidelity has been known to severely damage or destroy many good starts. My friends have told me that soon I'll start getting the itch to do the bedroom boogie with someone besides Becky. We've all heard the phrase "no matter how good lobster might taste, if you eat it every day, sooner or later you'll want to eat peanut butter and jelly just for something different."

I've been monogamous (or "monotonous" as the weekend party buddies say) for over a year now, and I'm happy with it. The one-nighters got old, and I like the additional pleasure that you feel during sex when you love the person that you're doing it with. Every time we have sex we both send juices a-flyin' because we know how to drive each other wild, and that makes the pursuit of the hot and heavy even better. If I ever do start to get bored with our sex I know that all I have to do is talk about it and we'll work it out just like we would any other problem. I don't need to go find someone else to get the thrill of variety.

Because of my commitment to my partner and my desire to take responsibility in the relationship, I feel no desire to betray Becky. In order to benefit from the good things that a woman brings you, you have to ward off the temptations from the bad. Certain situations may make that very challenging, but if you steadfastly resist it, the task becomes much easier. The best way to avoid putting yourself in a difficult position is to stay out of places and situations that are easy prey to pick someone up. Unless you are one of the few men who are either attractive or rich enough that women throw themselves at your feet at every turn, simply not looking to pick up women is the best way to avoid doing it. As the aggressors in male/female relationships we males have the benefit that most women will not actively pursue us if we show no interest. They do not have to be beaten over the head with a baseball bat to receive the "not interested" message as males do. But when you start flirting with and giving signals of interest to females who find you appealing you can get yourself into compromising situations. This is where that steadfast resistance thing comes in. If you never give impressions of sexual interest to other women your chances of actually scoring with one decreases rapidly.

My friends still think I'll soon start checking out the color of the grass on the other side because they have only my track record to go on. I must admit that given their knowledge of my life when having sex with the same girl two-nights in a row was the closest that I came to monogamy, I'd be a bit doubtful about my ability to hold myself back, too. But, now all that I have do to is look at everything that I have with Becky and say to myself "Is it worth risking all of that for one night of rolling around with someone different?" I spent many years looking for a relationship like this, and a year nurturing it, so where does five minutes of pleasure with some nobody fit into the big picture?

Then they give me the next scenario. What if you're out with the boys, she's not around and there's no way she'll find out about what you did. You've been sippin' a few cold ones, and some beautiful piece of flesh makes it just too easy for you to pick her up? Would you screw around on Becky under those circumstances? You can't make the situation more challenging to the concept of monogamy, especially to someone who previously had the sexual willpower of the average rabbit. But the answer is—no. This did happen to me, so I know this from personal experience.

A while back I was out with the boys having a couple of "pops" on a Friday night. During my fifth trip to the bar, I noticed a thin, attractive girl smiling at me, so during my time at the bar we shared some casual bar talk. After I got the drinks I said good-bye and thought that I had seen the last of her. Ten minutes later who taps me on the shoulder—little Ms. short, dark and easy. When I realized that her pants clearly had the "vacancy" sign flashing for me I was actually taken back for a second. My immediate thought was, where the hell was this girl during my sleazy days, but then, despite five beers worth of amnesia, my mind remembered Becky.

First I thought about how much I enjoyed my relationship and how much I did-n't want to hurt Becky. That was enough to make my decision, but I kept piling on other things just to show myself how dumb picking up this other girl would be (besides a drunk mind can never have too much reinforcement). I heaved the possi-bility of catching a venereal disease and giving it to Becky onto my emotional guilt pile. That would bring her about as much joy as terminal diarrhea. Finally, why spend all the time and effort pursuing horizontal push-ups with someone when the sex wouldn't be as good as what I'm used to. At the risk of sounding self-righteous, if people want to screw around on someone they love, more power to you. I've heard all of the rationalizations, justifications, and reasoning for getting naked and grunt-ing with another woman, and it's just something that I choose not to do. It's just not worth it. If you weigh the benefits versus the potential damage that it could cause you'll always come out with the same result. You heard it here. It's amazing the dif-ferences that love can make isn't it? When a relationship is good you'll make some serious changes in your life to keep it that way. But there are many other things that can make the love turn sour.

In the midst of a conversation with a friend of mine a while back he detailed how his relationship had done just that. His problem was not one of arguments, infidelity, or a lack of friendship, but instead it was one of a love that had faded into oblivion over time. He enjoyed her company more than anyone else's, but according to him he did not feel the same as he used to. Dr. Ruth would have a field day with this one.

The relationship had lost its spark, but the question was, could he get it back? If he felt it was worth salvaging and he was willing to adjust his mind set to do so, then it definitely could. What most likely happened was that the love and romance faded because they cut down on or stopped doing the things which kept that facet of the relationship flourishing. This has to be worked at just like anything else. Romantic dinners, candlelit back rubs, hand-in-hand walks through the woods. You need to do things on a regular basis that help you to maintain your romantic love. As people get comfortable and set into routines they sometimes forget about the romantic things that they did during the courtship phase. Those special things that helped you to fall in love in the first place can be used to rekindle the flame when it starts to smolder.

An adjustment to the way you think about romance must accompany these activ-ities. If you have written off the romance in your mind chances are that you won't be able to cultivate the emotions which will allow you to release your romantic feelings. It is much like when someone that you know is really annoying the crap out of you. They could say and do the exact things as someone you enjoy being with, but because of your biased predisposition against the person, their actions will continue to bother you until you change your mindset. That is why it is good to start with things that were romantic and pleasurable for you in the past. If you call up your memories to help jog your mind on what it feels like to share some romance with your partner, then you can more easily bridge the gap towards rejuvenating those feelings. If you do successfully re-establish these emotions remember to reinforce them by doing romantic things more frequently until you've totally rejuvenated your love.

How about this problem? A man says "After three years with the same woman I could kick Mike Tyson's butt for 15 rounds. I'm the best fighter I know." This isn't a healthy thing in any relationship, but couples are especially susceptible to verbal or, even worse, physical brawls. Sure she's going to piss you off over time—nobody's perfect. But why not exercise a bit of patience and self-control instead of going into a disagreement with your fists raised. If you strip off the attitude that "she'll always be there for me, why not use her as my emotional floor mat?" your relationship will be much better. The mentality of yell first, apologize later is outdated but still prevalent in today's society.

Especially in these times when people have a greater tendency to let their emotions fly you should be careful to control your emotions. Tired, drunk, and being stressed-out are all breeding grounds for the big blow-out, so use some extra caution in these situations. Take a deep breath, walk away or explain to her that you are feeling a bit out of it and that you'd rather talk about it when you feel a bit more level headed. An understanding partner will see that you are trying to keep things from escalating and will react accordingly. If she tries instead to provoke a conflict because she wants to fight, then the two of you should sit down at a time that isn't emotionally charged and establish the ground rules for how you'll avoid a fight in the future. This way you'll both be able to remind the other how to react when problems do arise, and it will install another barrier to the knock-down-drag-out fight. Anything that will help to keep these brawls from occurring will be a big plus.

You always hear people talking about how much violence and hatred there is in the world. A lot of it starts right in the home. People who have verbal tirades with their partner generate a great deal of anger that inevitably gets dumped on those around them. Even worse, it teaches their kids that if it is okay to treat the person that you love the most with irreverence and disrespect, and it must be okay to do the same to everyone else in the world. It follows then that disrespect for the law and your fellow man aren't too bad either. Verbal tirades and the anger that ensues from them serve to propagate the same rage and violence down to the next generation. Kids don't have those traits at birth, but Mom and Dad make great teachers. Just think about that before you lash-out.

Even before you settle down to the family life and control your rage for the kid's sake, do it for her sake, and do it for your own sake. How much do you enjoy being together right after a big blow-out? It takes a while for your adrenaline flow to get back to normal, and another couple of hours of your time is wasted stewing over the things that were said in the heat of the moment. Then you walk on egg shells for a while sharing conversation that is about as deep as a dried-up puddle to keep from further sparking the disagreement. Most of all, for the next few days you over-analyze every word she says in an attempt to gauge her level of forgiveness. The relationship is then put on hold until you both slowly repair the love and trust that the battle destroyed. One five-minute fight can produce scars that take anywhere from a few days to a lifetime to heal. Is it all worth it?

Instead, talk things out rationally, calmly and in a non-aggressive manner. You'll find that you'll accomplish a lot more while avoiding the residual effects of the big battles. Share with your partner how you feel and explain to her why her actions bother you. It is not only important to know what to say at these moments but how to say it. Remember, even if there aren't outward displays of rage, these moments are still very emotionally charged. Saying things in a harsh manner could easily ignite the situation. Talk slowly and use language that conveys your dissatisfaction, but do so in a way that is not belittling or provocative. During the conversation try adding in a few statements that show your understanding of her feelings and whenever possible explain situations which have caused you to feel the same way. This will make her feel less defensive and will also help keep you from sounding like you are directly attacking her. Also, having these talks while lying down beside her will help keep the situation more relaxed. Should it be an especially important discussion, sitting face-to-face will add some emphasis to the intensity of your emotions. After airing your feelings, come to a mutual decision about what changes will be made to keep the problem from reoccurring.

Establishing a step-by-step plan for solving the problem will help make the solution more concrete. If you have some pre-set guidelines which help you to avoid an undesired behavior, then it will be that much easier to do so. There are some personal changes that need to be mastered in order to conquer the fine art of "constructive crisis resolution," but when you do you will find it to be very beneficial to the relationship in the long-run. The more that you deal with your differences in this manner you'll find that "this ain't so hard" and you will have much more time to enjoy the good things that the relationship has to offer.

An unnecessary reason that people prefer the old "scream and ream" technique of dealing with problems is that it gives you the opportunity to manipulate your partner's future actions for your own personal gain. The frame of mind that frequently brings this about stems from the fact that in the heat of argument you can say anything you want and it will stick in her mind enough that you can manipulate her with it later. Forget about it. Take the politics out. Successful relationships are not manipulative.

Politics and mind games are the breeding grounds for frustration and anger. Successful relationships are not adversarial, nor do they strive to crown a victor while the loser wallows in defeat. Instead, these affiliations consist of two equal partners working side-by-side, doing things for the good of the relationship and not for selfish personal reasons.

The bottom line here is to have your partner at your side rather than under your thumb. Even if you do manage to find a woman who will allow you to keep her under lock and key, she will not feel fulfilled by the relationship and will never truly be happy. The old concept of "the man is king of his castle" is another of the outdated "caveman concepts." You'll get much more out of the relationship if both participants are happy and equal.

Yes, maintaining a love throughout a lifetime that is full of changes, difficulties, and differing personal goals is one of the most challenging things that we humans are faced with. Hence the reason for those sad statistics that began this chapter. But it is not impossible. A few months ago I spoke to a man and woman who were in the midst of celebrating their 50th wedding anniversary. After noticing that they were still very much in love I asked them what they felt were the most important things that I, as someone much their junior in the love department, could do to reach their point. They both agreed that even though communication and always resolving their differences without major fights were important in avoiding fall-outs, what really made their relationship a happy one was taking the time each day to remember their fond memories of the past, and then spending even more time focusing on creating new ones. I thought about that for a while that night, and though it seemed simple, being able to accomplish this over a 50-year period is quite remarkable. It left a target for Becky and me to shoot for. If we could do what that couple did I am sure that my life with Becky will be a happy one.

Officially Living Together:
The Toilet Seat's Always Down

Cohabitation and All of Its Finer Points

The bathroom is where it all happens. Sure, she might add some flowers or other female touches to the other rooms of the house, but it's the bathroom where it first hits you that "I'm actually doing it, I'm living with my girlfriend!" The refrigerator-sized box labeled "Bathroom Stuff" that I carried from the truck when she moved in was a tip-off, but when I first saw 3,000 bottles, jars, and cans strewn about the bathroom—that's when I came to the realization that life as I knew it would never be the same.

I was sitting on the throne one day soon after Becky moved in with me. She had thrown out the *Playboy* magazine that was my usual bathroom reading material, so out of sheer boredom I started looking around at all of the junk that was scattered around what used to be my bathroom. After pondering the usefulness of this seemingly worthless stuff, I said to myself "How many thousands of dollars a year does she spend on this junk?" I could get season tickets for next year's football season and have money left over for vacation just on what she spends for her bathroom beautifiers. Liquid body lufra, moisturizing mud, bath geleé—does this stuff actually have a purpose or is it just a great marketing scheme by the cosmetics companies designed to suck whole paychecks out of the population's female half?

Besides the bathroom, some more subtle changes have come into place since my roommates departed from the wayward home for single men and were replaced by Becky. The feminine decorating ideas that she takes such pride in can be seen in every room. I won't admit it to my friends, but I like her decor much better than my standard male fare. For the first time ever my place of residence looks more like a home than a locker room. There must be a special interior decorating gene in a woman's DNA that men don't have. Men in turn get the map reading gene that women don't have. It's a trade off. More likely, maybe men just don't care about the quality of their decor enough to labor for hours over a dried flower arrangement in a wicker basket. Whatever the case may be, the place looks a lot better and it didn't cost me a dime. So who am I to complain? She's not the perfect interior designer, though. A couple of her decorating ideas looked like they came from *Better Barnyards and Gardens* magazine. To avoid hurting her feelings I quickly became well-versed in the art of "constructive compromise." As a reward for my endeavors her pink-framed Mother Goose picture found it's way into a closet in the spare bedroom without bringing about any ill-feelings.

I am starting to learn that the art of compromise is one of the most important aspects of sharing your dwelling with the woman you love. Once you bring her into the fold your time and choices are not strictly your own any more. From simple things like what to eat for dinner, to complex decisions like what kind of furniture to buy, spontaneous whims of choice have been replaced by discussion and compromise. Having to explain and justify my reasoning for the things that I used to do impetuously provides me with an added challenge. Now I have to give the reason why I prefer to wait until a layer of sedimentary rock forms on my dishes before I wash them, or why I pay my bills a week late even when I have the money to pay them on time. But we all have stupid or lazy things that we do. And luckily for my male ego, I get to point out some of hers from time to time. At any rate, you both get the opportunity to teach the other a few things about every day life which help you to become more productive. You also learn to compromise for the sake of making everyday life pass more smoothly than Metamucil meatloaf, and you both will benefit from this.

I found these compromises started cutting into my daily free time, and that started to worry me. After a few weeks of feeling that I went from a straight-A student to a perennial flunky in the School of Leisure Time Accomplishment I asked myself "What are you doing with your free time now? Yeah, we are having more sex now, but not four hours a day." Is my free time kicking back with Gilligan and the Skipper on some uncharted desert isle? Where the hell did it go? So I sat back and analyzed my new nightly routine—there the answer lies. She hasn't mastered the fine art of time management for life's trivialities as I have, and it is causing me to compromise some of my time.

Take cooking for instance. Doesn't she know that the improved taste of a meal achieved through using 4 pans, 3 bowls, and a tried and true recipe doesn't compare to throwing the ingredients in one bowl simultaneously and saving 30 minutes cooking time and six dirty dishes? Julia Child may beg to differ but pasta doesn't taste any different if you wait until the water boils before you throw the spaghetti in the pan. Vegetables—that's what a microwave is for.None of this steaming them over boiling water to retain the nutrients. Why should I take multi-vitamins if I'm getting my daily supply of the 14 essentials from my green beans? A few weeks into the living together routine was all that it took for me to learn that arriving home from my nightly workout just before she finished making dinner was the perfect way to avoid the whole cooking ordeal. Continuing in the spirit of compromise, I did the dishes as a way of showing my appreciation for her hard work. My idea for paper plates and plastic silverware following my first dish-cleaning duty didn't fly, but hey—she can't blame me for trying.

Dinner hour is not the only place that you lose time. Before this stage of our relationship I would meet her at her apartment at a time which allowed me some leeway for my daily rituals and a bit of relaxation. Now that time is in the archives. This took me a while to adjust to. I need some time to be alone, lay on the couch, and mellow out after a hard day. In order to do this now I've had to develop some female proof methods. I've learned that if you walk into the bathroom with the newspaper under your arm you will make it through the sports section, and whatever other parts of the paper you would like to read, without the slightest fear of interruption. My scientific studies have revealed that 19 minutes is about the maximum time that you can sit on the toilet before your legs start to fall asleep.

Getting the rest of the body to sleep for the night is a whole different story. Sleep, that eight-hour sanctuary which provides you with an unconscious respite from the real world, comes to a crashing halt when she crawls into bed with me 20 minutes after I've been pounding Zs. It starts with her simple desire to cuddle. At this point I want nothing more than to continue with the dream that was rudely interrupted a couple minutes back, but I must fulfill a quota of kisses before returning to my happy state of unconscious. Little do I realize that those few half-awake kisses start her down the path of sexual craving and my attempts to get some precious REMs will be futile until she is sexually satiated for the evening. Her head going southward on my body meets with no resistance on my end, and I go from semi-conscious to sexually standing at attention in no time. I'm not complaining. Sleep is a small price to pay to end the day in such a grand fashion. Yet after the completion of our sexual endeavors I realize that despite a high rating on the pleasure scale, I've successfully lost another hour of my day.

As for the other lost moments, daily routines, and relaxation, I broke down and explained to her that I would like a bit of time each evening to do my own thing before sharing the remainder of the evening with her. Surprisingly, Becky was glad that I suggested this because she felt that she was missing this same thing. After that, things worked out a lot better. I take about an hour to be a lazy leech by myself, and afterwards we do things together—what more could a man ask for?

Here was another of those times that talking about the little problems that we encounter in the relationship proved to be beneficial for both of us. It is especially important to do this when you start living together because outside of work you are together just about every moment of the day. In the pre-shack-up days if you needed some time to be alone you could retreat back to your own abode for a relationship "coffee-break," but that option no longer exists. Now you either have to face the situation or take the easy way out and get yourself a couple of hobbies that give you some time apart. Maybe that's why married guys get greasy hobbies that are guaranteed not to remotely interest their wives. By the time you're married you've had plenty of time to perfect the art of getting some moments to yourself. No wonder married guys spend so much time cutting the lawn. I guess that finding the proper balance of time spent together and apart to ensure that both people are satisfied takes a lot of practice. This is just another one of those things we have to learn through personal experience in order to make cohabitation successful.

Learning to budget and enjoy your time both with and without each other is important because the more time that you spend with any person, the more the potential exists for problems to arise between you. Even petty annoyances can build into major arguments if you allow them to. That is why non-offensive conversation about your differences becomes so essential. I've found that mentioning one of our similarities or something that I enjoy about living together prior to delving into what she did that bothered me is a good way to avoid those "claws-out-cat-fight" type of battles.

This experience has also taught me that you must have added patience and a give-and-take mentality to keep the relationship moving forward when you are shacking-up. When I noticed that a couple of little things that she did were trying my patience, I thought to myself, this is the person that you hope to spend the rest of your life with. Maybe a little extra slack is deserved here. I also thought back to my roommate during my freshman year of college who was my best friend at the time. In only one semester we went from blood brothers to the verge of drawing blood. I think it all stemmed from a disagreement over a box of macaroni and cheese or something equally as earth shattering, but the point is that it is very difficult to live with anyone. This difficulty increases exponentially the closer that you are to the person. I've found that most people have a tendency to take the people closest to them for granted. When someone feels that you are not giving them the common courtesy that you would any other person they feel hurt and disappointed. In any close relationship people need to feel that you respect them as much as you do yourself. If you are not giving them this respect it will tend to piss them off relatively easily. The moral of the story is to exercise more patience than normal with your live-in. And if you find that your concerns continue over a period of time, talk to her about it and try to eliminate the problem. Yeah, I know, I'm beating this give-and-take thing into the ground but it is so important that I feel I must. Remember if you have a thoughtful partner the more you give the more you will get in return. Though the saying goes that it is better to give than receive, receiving makes a pretty damn good reward for giving.

I realized this at the beginning of football season. In our incipient beginnings last year I sacrificed most of my Sunday game-watching to be with Becky. I found out quickly that catching late night highlights just didn't cut it. On opening day this year who would have thought that she would actually suggest that I go watch the games with four or five other fanatic friends at my favorite satellite-equipped bar. She gave me an open invitation to go slug a few back with the boys and male bond like the old days. All right, what's the catch here? Knowing that she likes football about as much as she enjoys bricks crashing from three stories high into her skull, why did she suggest that I go spend my entire Sunday watching it? What was I missing? I thought about it for a second; then I began to understand her reasoning. It was simple—she loves me. She knew that I love football, and she was willing to sacrifice some of our time together in order to make me happy. I asked her about it and she confirmed my thoughts. Let me tell you, this love thing can be downright cool sometimes. All of the fringe benefits of the relationship and football too. What a deal.

At that moment I had one of those emotion-filled moments, said "The Words," and gave her a big hug and a long kiss. I didn't even start the mental planning process of who I was going to call to watch the games. I was simply engulfed in feelings of love. My emotions didn't even have anything to do with football per se (well at least not much). It was simply that she cared for me so much that she wanted me to be happy, even if it did mean being apart for the day. Thinking more about someone else's needs than your own, and reaping the rewards when they do the same, I tell you that this give-and-take can be a good thing. More and more I'm finding that it plays an integral role in the making of a successful relationship.

I was so overcome with feelings of love that I wondered why there aren't more times that I take notice of the things that she does for me and how much I enjoy our relationship. People have a tendency to take the good in life for granted while noticing the faults and the bad elements in personal relationships. Why don't we change this so that our focus is to revel in and enjoy the good times while downplaying and working through the bad times? Yes, it is easier to notice the negative emotions in life because of the strong responses that they elicit in our mind and body. But anger, hatred, and fear aren't the only emotions that can take over your mind. Love can do the same. We don't live for the bad things that happen to us in life; we live for the good. We have to expect bad experiences to occur in our lives, but why not deal with them quickly and constructively so that we can focus our mind on a state in which it is receptive to the good. The people in this world that can do this are the truly happy ones. The people that focus on being pissed off and looking for the bad things in others will surely find it.

Maybe that is why Becky and I are so happy. We try to look for the good in each other, and even in the difficult times we get the negative emotions out so that we can get back to the ready state of happiness. This process of working through our problems serves to make me appreciate our relationship even more. Sharing the same living quarters has made our bond stronger and has moved me one step closer to the point where I could conceive of taking the matrimonial plunge. I'm not cruising the local jewelry stores just yet, but who knows, it may be happening in the near future.

Through our experiences I have seen that living together gives you a pre-marriage compatibility testing ground. You wouldn't think of buying a car without test driving it, so why shouldn't you do the same with the most important investment in your life? I never thought of cohabitation as a make it or break it type of situation, but I guess that is what it boils down to. If you find that the additional pressures of living together reveal some problems in the relationship that could never be solved, then why commit yourself to a lifetime of frustration because of them. Why not find this out before you have to endure the emotional, financial, and legal headaches of a divorce? I think that many of the under two year annulments could be avoided if everyone spent six months under the same roof prior to engagement. Society has finally gotten to the point in which "living in sin" isn't cause to be ostracized, so why not get the added assurance that your relationship can handle the full-time commitment prior to making it?

Living together also may produce other benefits down the road. The first thing that many couples do in post-nuptial life is to push out a puppy. Some even do so after their relationship gets a bit rocky thinking that a child will help bring them back together. If you are not compatible before having the child, chances are that changing dirty diapers and waking-up to a crying baby at 4 a.m. isn't going to make things "all better." After the initial euphoria of the birth and having a family wears off the problems in the relationship that you experienced before the child was born will reappear. This will compound your problems because now you must consider the child's needs and take responsibility for them for the remainder of your life.

Even though some people still consider living together prior to marriage a moral outrage, I think it is a necessity. I am glad that Becky and I have done it because the things that I've learned will help to make our life together happier, and it gave me peace of mind in knowing that we are compatible when sharing the same roof. It certainly has made those thoughts of the big M word happening sometime soon a bit less frightening.

Married?

An Experience 'Til Death Do Us Part

The stage was set. The arrangements had been made. It was planned to perfection—there was no way that things could go awry. A moment like this is once in a lifetime. It was the night that would change two lives forever. But he had to remain calm. He could show no signs of stress. Screwing this one up would be like serving steak tar-tar at a Hindu dinner party.

It was February 14th, a cool wintry day that couldn't make up its mind between sunshine and dreary. He picked her up promptly at 2 p.m. The arrival alluded to the importance of the day. He was not in his car, but instead he arrived via stretch limousine. She could not contain her excitement and surprise. "This is special. This is so romantic," she said to him. The oversized Cadillac transported them to a four-star restaurant 10 miles outside of town. When the driver opened the door to find the two of them in the midst of a deep kiss, he wasn't surprised. It was obvious that these two were very much in love.

All throughout dinner she noticed an unending glow upon the face of the one she loved. He was secretly hoping that she didn't figure out what was about to transpire. After a delicious meal and an accompanying bottle of wine, they walked out of the restaurant arm-in-arm and heard the sound of a small plane flying overhead. A gasp of amazement overcame her as she saw the words "Marry Me" spelled out in the afternoon sky. The plane then swooped low and the pilot flung a small balloon into the air. Hanging from the balloon was a string with a diamond dangling at it's end. As she reached her arm up to catch it, the diamond landed into her outstretched hand. The gold band fit perfectly onto her ring finger. Her ensuing hugs and kisses almost knocked him to the ground. She could barely contain her joy. As for the tears, she wasn't as able to hold them back. It looked like a faucet had been opened in her eyes. There they stood in the parking lot for 10, 15 minutes maybe, but neither had any concept of time. Love was the only thing they thought about. It might have lasted longer, but the limousine pulled up behind them and they swiftly returned to reality. They floated in their cloud of love for the entire ride home, only to pause briefly to talk about forever and of living happily ever after.

Does all of this sound like a fairy tale? All right, maybe it was more like a dime-store novel, but at any rate that was my description of how I envisioned popping the question to Becky. After a year and a half of dating I was sure about the feelings that I had from the beginning. She was the person that I wanted to spend my life with.

My actual Valentine's Day proposal did go pretty much according to the plan. Yeah, she might have had suspicions of what was occurring prior to my asking, and we had to chase the balloon a couple hundred yards before finally catching up to it. But other than that, the night was perfect. By the time the limo dropped us back home, I was overwhelmed with love for the woman who would soon be taking my name.

When we got out of the limo we spent a few more minutes wrapped up in each other. That lasted until she felt the need to fulfill her excited bride-to-be requirement by proceeding at light speed to every friend, neighbor, and relative's house. She spent the rest of the evening showing off the new rock that adorned her ring finger, sharing some happiness, and shedding a couple of tears. As for me, I decided to stay behind and ponder the new direction to which my compass of life now pointed.

There I stood in my yard on a cool winter evening, gazing out at my neighborhood as some of Mom Nature's white stuff slowly descended upon me. The wintry scene before me slowly faded as the image of the Friday night crowd at Big Boppers gained control of my mind's picture tube. The usuals were all there—"grandma," the bar-maid who made drinks at toxic strength, and a few of my drunken woman-hunting friends. But something was different. Instead of being perched on my usual step at the bar's upper level, I was staring at the scene through the window, looking in from the outside at the things I used to live for. When I looked away from the window I felt a chill going up my spine and snow blanketing my hair as I stood outside the bar. Soon the picture faded and I found myself again staring at the clouds of a February evening. Back to my home in suburbia—back to the present.

Those bar days were the most fun that I've ever experienced. Even though I wouldn't want to go back, I can't help but reminisce about the babes, booze, and bar-rooms in the days of the 6 a.m. bedtime. I now realize just how much different my lifestyle has become. Yes, a year and a half ago that was me trudging through the crowd to find a woman to ease my loneliness for the night. But now I have passed the torch to someone else. A younger, more virile guy who is still willing to tolerate the hangovers, numerous rejections, and the nights going home to an empty bed is prob-ably there on my old step displaying the same persistence and chip on his shoulder that I once had.

I, on the other hand, have aspired to a new plane, one at which it is acceptable to stay home on a Friday night if I'm not into the social scene; one at which I feel a new-found stability and sense of direction in my life; most of all, one at which a best friend, a lover, and a roommate all rolled into one has risen above all else to become the most important part of my life.

I am at the beginning of the next phase of my life. It is a bit more tame, but it is still very enjoyable. Now don't get me wrong, I haven't become a parishioner of the Church of the Constipated Excitement, and I haven't even considered playing in a bridge tournament. I still go to parties and bars like the old days, but now I don't view getting blasted as a prerequisite to having a good time, and I have a girl with me who I know will sleep with me at the end of the night. I find that I still have about the same amount of fun. I've simply chopped off some of the extreme peaks and valleys. There may be fewer of those raucous split-your-gut fun times, but gone are the lonely nights and the Sunday mornings with only a hangover and an empty wallet to show for my weekend endeavors.

Occasionally I go out for a few cold ones with some of my old drinking buddies who are also in the process of readying themselves to say "I do." Whenever I see them the conversation inevitably leads us back to the days of old. Eventually we start talking about our current situations and we take comfort from knowing that someone else from the party crew has climbed the relationship ladder at the same pace that we have. This serves to reaffirm our knowledge that despite a much different lifestyle from days past, we are indeed following the right paths for our future. During this conversation we ponder the good qualities of our current relationships and come away from the experience feeling a couple of notches better about ourselves and our newly charted courses. If in the process we get into a spontaneous "my Dad is bigger than your Dad" boastfest about our partners and our relationships at least we know that our competitive side still exists and that it can carry over to even the most trivial aspects of life.

In the end one person inevitably asks "Do you ever want to go back?" We both delay a second, then simultaneously look at each other and answer "Of course!" I think that every man who has ever lived and loved the party scene misses it at times. Every now and then that grass on the other side looks "oh so green." How can anything compare to living your life with the Id of a kid, doing whatever you want with no regard for anyone but yourself and your friends, and shirking life's responsibilities whenever possible. As far as unbridled fun goes, those were definitely the days, and everyone likes to think back to a simpler time every now and then.

But when asked if we want to trade in our current lifestyle to go back the old, the tune goes from Guns 'N Roses to Bach in no time. "Nah, no thanks. It's fun to do those things once in a while, but not all the time." It's like the evolution from ape to man all over again. It's definitely different, but in the grand scheme of things it's better. We see many differences and changes in ourselves, but we know that we are happier because of them.

There is a lot more to it, though. Now I feel that I am a better person. I treat myself and the people around me with more kindness and respect. I feel that I am nicer because of the happiness that Becky has brought to me. Nice. Just saying that word sends a Pavlovian chill through the bones of this dog. I think back to the sluttin' days when "you're nice" was the kiss of death from a girl. I used to habitually reply "I'm far from nice, but I'm a hell of a lot of fun. Just wait and see." Men who were nice got laid with the same regularity of a mouse in a lion's cage. But now I'm "nice" and she loves me. Maybe it's a boost to her ego that she helped me to become a nicer person, who knows? Whatever the effect it has on her, I know that I do treat people with more kindness and respect because of her. I don't feel as though I have to prove myself to her. Yet sometimes when I go the extra mile to help someone out, or when I realize some negative traits that I have curbed since I met her, I know that I did so partly for her. I do it so she can see the good in me, and be happy with who I am. She is proud of me and she's proud to be with me, and I continually strive to make her proud.

One of Becky's influences that I've noticed is that I'm more in tune with the world around me. Men have a tendency to block out situations and people that don't directly relate to them, whereas woman absorb what is going on around them much more. Now I notice the homeless man on the street and feel bad for him, and I will go out of my way to get the door for an old woman. But even though I do more nice things and feel more for other people, that is not the most important thing for her. Women have a thing about motives. Helping the old lady with the hope that she'll give you something in return doesn't wash. The action counts, but it is the reason behind it that matters to a woman. It took me a while to realize that one, but eventually it sunk in. I found that the more things that I did for others, not only did I feel better about myself, but it started becoming second nature. Now I do things for others to make them feel better. To see a smile or hear a "thank you" is more rewarding than giving yourself a pat on the back.

In return for my efforts not only has Becky learned from and made changes for me, but she is also there to console me when life hovers ever near the proverbial crapper. She knows me almost as well as I know myself. She is there for me to empathize with yet also to instruct. Knowing that she will be there to guide me through the rough spots makes facing life's challenges much easier. Having a person who helps you release your self-doubt and anxieties definitely raises your tolerance level for dealing with life's pains. Where most people might start to get sick of hearing about your problems, a lover is always there for you and will do whatever is necessary to help you resolve the situation. This allows you to strive for greater personal growth by providing you with the strength and perseverance to try things that you would normally not attempt.

The stability that your partner gives you will by no means ensure your success, but having some added resources in your corner certainly gives you a better chance of winning the fight. It is much like the feeling that I got when going on vacation soon after having a burglar alarm installed in my house. The additional security and peace of mind that the alarm gave me prior to leaving home allowed me to travel through my days without the anxieties and fears that I had before. It didn't guarantee that when I came home that my house wouldn't be stripped bare of everything worth 10 cents or more, but it certainly decreased the chances and allowed me to worry about it much less.

I have a friend who started a small printing company when he was in his early twenties and built it into a successful national corporation. He weathered the storms of many difficulties along the way, but through every step his girlfriend (who later became his wife) stood beside him. I won't be so bold as to say that he wouldn't have made it without her, but I know that through the many setbacks that his business and his personal life suffered she was there to help him through the problems. Sometimes that meant slaving with him late into the night. Other times she provided him with a sounding board for new ideas, and on many occasions she would simply hold him in her arms until he found himself soothed, relaxed, and able to face the next day. When his success finally arrived he thanked and attributed it to her strength and influence.

As individuals we all have maximum levels of endurance for pain, rejection, and failure. Though these levels differ from person to person, our resistance to them increases when given the opportunity to vent these problems by tapping into the well of a partner's consolation. What better source is there from which to water your dreams of success than someone who will provide you with love, guidance, and strength to endure life's hardships? Even the worst hitter will eventually hit a home run if he gets to the plate enough times. It is our own fear of failure that keeps us from doing the things that help make us successful. And a lack of perseverance can cause us to quit when what we are striving for is just around the corner. Someone who will provide us with the security and stability to go the distance can be the difference between a lifetime of happiness and one of frustration from climbing a mountain of unfulfilled goals. When you find someone who gives you this personal strength, hold on with two hands because she will definitely help you to change your life for the better.

Yes, she will change you. When I look back at my life before Becky, I realize that I've made a whole load of personal alterations. If a couple of years ago I looked at "today's me" I would have been forced to decide whether "wimp" or "pussy" best described my current state of being. I'm more like a fine wine now than the "Chateau of the Month" that I used to be—I've definitely mellowed with age. I'm happy about that. Even though I used to wish that the endless partying would never come to a halt, now I can't see myself as a gray-haired, 50-year-old scouring the bingo halls for available babes. Now fixing the sink or raking the leaves seems to be easier to visualize. Even though the latter definitely sounds like a much less enjoyable alternative, as we move through life the concept of stability and all that comes with it seems to be a better option than the constant action of the singles life. I find that I haven't lost my zest for excitement and fulfillment, I've just changed the activities that provide me with those sensations. Activities like golfing, tropical vacations, and attending cultural events have replaced playing football, drunken road trips, and picking up women as my standard fare. Though part of the change can be attributed to my increased financial means as I get older most of it is due to the fact that the body and the mind needed something different. Even on those rare occasions that the whole gang assembles for a night's revelry we leave feeling that it was a good time, and at the same time we wonder how we ever did that five nights a week.

Instead, it is usually a few couples getting together for dinner that brings this once inseparable clan back together. Most of them are already married, and since I will be in their ranks shortly I'm sure that we'll see each other even less. After our wives start popping out the puppies I'd even venture a guess that we'll see each other much less than the couple of times a month that we currently get together. From spending five nights a week together to twice a month in just two years, that's quite a change. I guess that as your priorities in life change so does the allocation of your time with the people around you. I know that I enjoy spending time with Becky more than with my friends, so I am happy about the change. The guys realize that we haven't abandoned each other and that our friendships are still important even if we don't spend the same amount of time together. But you can't help but feel differently now given the numerous changes we've all undergone.

Now we cram a month's worth of catching up into a few hour period at happy hour, or by talking through a hoops game. Yet we still enjoy each other's company as much as we used to. Actually now that we're not pursuing numerous females and amassing endless stories every weekend, this short period of time is about all that we need to keep up with our friend's latest happenings. It seems that a house and a spouse doesn't leave us much time to get soused. Responsibility—it's a part of getting older and a part of growing up. It happened to our parents. It's happening to us, and someday it will happen to our kids.

But I'm still the same person underneath these heaps of responsibility. I didn't trade-in my old self for a new one, I just made some trade-offs. Like any other phase of your life it is what you make of it that counts. I may not have the freedom that I used to, but I can still enjoy myself and feel happy about my life. That is why it is so important that the woman that you marry is the right person for you, and is not just someone who you settle for because your friends have all disappeared. She's the one who is going to be with you more than anyone, she will be mother to your children and be there when you retire and start tooling around the country in an RV. So make the right choice. I feel that I've found the perfect person for me in Becky, and I am readying myself to move on to the next level with her. Though I never thought I'd hear myself say this, "Bring on the wedding bells, I am ready."

Alas the big day had finally arrived. All the wedding planning and gory details that quickly became more and more tedious were behind us, and my daily planner for the day simply said "Get married." Although the first few hours of the day consisted of fulfilling some preparatory obligations they seemed much less tedious than I would have thought they would be. The herd of friends that I forced into tuxes to help me enjoy the day certainly helped this out. I couldn't help but feel a bit of nervousness because of the importance and symbolism of the day. It was strange that even though I'd worn this same outfit numerous times for the weddings of the same friends gathered around me, it was a completely different situation being the one who was saying "I do."

But this shouldn't be any big thing, should it? Besides the legal pooling of assets and a wild shindig, the next day Becky and I would wake-up as the same two people deeply in love with each other, right? It's the mental stigma that changes things. My married friends have told me that you feel different about the relationship once you wear that band around your finger. There's a new sense of permanence that you feel after the nuptials, they say. The thought of "that's it, it's over" doesn't cross your mind after a serious disagreement. It is instead replaced by the thought that the relationship is going to last for the rest of our lives, so let's work things out. At least that's what they tell me. I had to wait until the completion of the day to find this out first hand.

That was in the back of my mind as the excitement of the occasion held my thoughts captive. It felt good. Maybe it was the euphoria of the whole event causing some weird chemical reactions in my brain, but it felt right. I didn't feel the burden of the responsibilities of what I was about to undertake. Maybe I was just Mr. Domestic waiting to happen while I was busy running around in the party guy costume for most of my adult life, but I felt totally confident about the events that were about to transpire. They say that I was supposed to have this severe case of frozen feet on that day, but my toes were not cold at all. It was because I knew that out of all of the thousands of girls that I had met in my life, the hundreds that I had some sort of interest in, the 50 or so that I had slept with, and the handful that I had been in love with, this girl was the one with whom I felt that I could best spend the rest of my days.

So as I stood there watching this beautiful woman dressed in white walking up an aisle between a roomful of people doing their best Japanese-tourist impersonations, I couldn't help but feel overcome with emotion. I was happy that I had found the person who made me feel whole. I was enamored with a woman that I cared for more than anyone else, and I was ecstatic about the prospect of feeling this way for the rest of my life. I knew that I would look back at this moment when things get rough and be able to draw from these emotions and from the experiences that brought us here. It reminded me of what the woman at her 50th wedding anniversary said about being able to remember these moments while striving each day to create new ones. That day was the beginning of a new chapter of my life's book. Though I had enjoyed the novel up to that point I looked toward the remainder with excitement about the experiences that life would offer me with the woman I love.

As she arrived by my side at the altar I saw that same beautiful smile that first attracted me to her from across the crowded bar way back when, and it made me think one last time about my past escapades, conquests, and unsuccessful relationships. I then realized that all of the sexual encounters and dating rituals, though very important to me at one time, seemed trivial compared to the way that I felt about my new life with the woman at my side.

About the Author

Peter Bartula was born into a nomadic Latvian family of gypsy sheep-herders who were Maytag repairpeople on the side. Eventually, his father found a niche as the man who sticks his head in the lion's mouth in a little known circus, and moved the family to the U.S. After 6 years of college where he majored in "Barley/Hops Engineering," Bartula entered the working world and obtained a part-time night job hanging out at bars and putting his degree to use. These life experiences gave him the expertise needed to create this book. Bartula offers these words of advice to his readers: "Remember that the dating world may have its downside, but some day you'll be married with screaming kids and a mortgage that you can't afford—so live every night like it is your last."